BR
115
H84
V36
1991

The Sense of Humor In Scripture, Theology And Worship

By Lee van Rensburg

COLORADO CHRISTIAN UNIVERSITY
LIBRARY
180 S. GARRISON
LAKEWOOD, COLORADO 80226

Fairway Press
Lima, Ohio

THE SENSE OF HUMOR
IN SCRIPTURE, THEOLOGY AND WORSHIP

FIRST EDITION
Copyright © 1991 by
Lee van Rensburg

All rights reserved. No portion of this book may be reproduced or utilized in any form or by any means, electronic or mechanical including photocopying, without permission in writing from the publisher. Inquiries should be addressed to: Fairway Press, 628 South Main Street, Lima, Ohio 45804.

7753 / ISBN 1-55673-300-3   PRINTED IN U.S.A.

Dedicated to my wife, Bronwyn,
and my three children,
Shaun, Deon, and Caryn,
whose quick recognition of our
family's many incongruities
provides the humorous perspective
that keeps us together.

FOREWORD

This short book is based on a Doctor of Ministry project undertaken by the author at his church in Whitehouse, New Jersey. The first section is a distilation of the main areas of thought in the intriguing and rewarding area of humor and Christian faith and is painted in broad strokes to give the reader an easy yet concise introduction to the subject. For the reader already familiar with this fruitful study area, the book serves as a useful precis. The first section draws liberally from many and varied sources and I express my gratitude to publishers and authors who so readily granted permission to quote from their pioneering work.

The second section is designed for practical use in worship and ministry. It contains many resources including litanies, prayers, hymn and Scripture suggestions as well as short sermon outlines for use in a Sunday worship service. These, when used with discretion, will enhance the worship experience and introduce a new dimension. This section also contains useful data for those who might wish to set up a humor profile for their church. These materials are easily adaptable and will be useful in any denomination or congregational size. They may be used verbatim or changed at discretion.

I express my sincere thanks to those of the D. Min. program of Drew University who guided my project; to the members and friends of the Whitehouse United Methodist Church who were game to go along with it often providing their own comical insights; to my two secretaries Judith Gutowski and Christine Krinis who not only typed, proofread, and efficiently dealt with the work involved in preparing a manuscript, but also provided tea, therapy and good common sense; to my friend Woody Bond who drew the rose window logo for the cover and Susan Marino for her help in choosing typeface for the cover title. Also, to the team at Fairway Press for their encouragement and insights in transforming a dissertation into a book.

May your church discover the spiritual strength that humor can release into your fellowship, learning, worship, ministry, and organizational structure. It is a unique, disarming and graceful gift from above.

Lee van Rensburg
Whitehouse, New Jersey
Easter 1991

TABLE OF CONTENTS

Introduction   9

CHAPTER 1 — HUMOR IN THE SCRIPTURE   17
    The Torah
    History and Psalms
    The Prophets
    Life and Ministry of Jesus
    Irony in the Fourth Gospel and Paul

CHAPTER 2 — HUMOR AND THEOLOGY   32
    Humor and the Creator
    The Imago Dei
    Humor and the Fall
    Humor and Redemption
    Humor and Compassion in Christ
    Human Nature of Christ
    The Trinity
    Towards a Theology of Humor

CHAPTER 3 — HUMOR IN THE SERVICE OF MINISTRY   45
    Humor and the Healing Ministry
    Humor and the Preaching Ministry
    Humor and Education
    Humor and Spiritual Growth

CHAPTER 4 — WORSHIP RESOURCES   54
    Litanies
    The Fool's Prayer
    Appropriate Hymns
    Scripture Passages
    Sermon Suggestions
    Humor Programs

CHAPTER 5 — A HUMOR PROFILE FOR YOUR CHURCH 80
    How to set up a humor profile
    Evaluation forms

APPENDIX 89

BIBLIOGRAPHY 92

INTRODUCTION

For many people, humor and the comic spirit is little more than frivolity — a refreshing moment that brings laughter, a release of tension, and a momentary sense of well being to be enjoyed and then almost immediately forgotten. That humor should have any further significance than this is not always recognized. However, laughter is only the tip of the humor iceberg; and below the surface lies the greater part of the dynamics and dimensions of humor. It is the hidden part of humor that is often thoughtful, logical, therapeutic, revelatory, and at times, aggressive and wounding, releasing both positive and negative forces into the individual or group that have profound and long lasting effects. To begin to perceive and understand these subtle yet significant effects of humor is to gain a new appreciation of the role humor has in our lives, to be challenged to be more circumspect as to what is happening to oneself, as well as to develop a more responsible and mature use of humor.

Psychologists and those who study humor seriously have long sought to produce an adequate theory of humor. This has proven to be an elusive task. In much the same manner that one loses the frog when the frog is dissected, so also the humorous element in a situation or story tends to dissipate when one attempts to define it. It is like the proverbial explaining of a joke — once this project is embarked upon, the joke is no longer funny.

Influential theories on humor have been offered by Bergson, Koestler, and Freud and provide us with a working introduction for our project. Bergson's essay on laughter immediately recognizes that the comic spirit cannot be imprisoned in a formula. It is too powerful and creative a force to be subject to simple definition. Bergson observes that laughter is a peculiarly human attribute, social in its orientation (requiring an echo), and that laughter is normally accompanied by the absence of feeling. The essence of laughter, for Bergson, lies in the tendency of people to lapse into mechanical or automatic acts that easily become habits, giving the impression that the body is being manipulated from outside as a puppet on a string. It is when something mechanical is encrusted on something living that laughter results. "Rigidity is the comic, and laughter is the corrective."[1] For Bergson,

> *The attitudes, gestures and movements of human body are laughable in exact proportion as the body reminds us of a mere machine.*[2]
>
> *To imitate anyone is to bring out the element of automatism he (sic) has allowed to creep into his person. And as this is the very essence of the ludicrous, it is no wonder that imitation gives rise to laughter.*[3]

Life — the spirit — should remain free and not have to repeat itself. When life fails to resist the temptation towards the mechanical or the habit, it is this very deflection toward the mechanical that is the cause of laughter. Bergson cites categories that particularly lend themselves to illustrating his theory, such as the ceremonial side of social life, the stereotypical, professional customs, fixed ideas, and the body following that which is natural (e.g. sneezes) while the spirit is attempting to maintain its composure in some other manner. A good example of the tendency to lapse into the mechanical is illustrated in Bergson's story . . .

> *Twenty years ago, a large steamer was wrecked off the coast at Dieppe. With considerable difficulty some of the passengers were rescued in a boat. A few custom-house officials who had courageously rushed to their assistance, began by asking them "if they had anything to declare."*[4]

Thus Bergson contends that "We laugh every time a person gives the impression of being a thing."[5]

Koestler finds the essence of laughter in what he terms bisociation. By this term he means the association of two normally non-related ideas that are brought together in an unexpected and unanticipated manner and given a logical intersection point. Thus we have the intersection of "two self-consistent but habitually incompatible frames of reference"[6] which often results in a reversal of logic as the following examples indicate: a convict was playing cards with his jailers, but on discerning that he was cheating they kicked him out of jail; the sadist who was being kind to a masochist! The bisociative act connects two different planes of thought with a common ground and the clash of these two planes, each logical in its own right, causes the explosion of laughter, or the comic effect. In the bisociation there is an abrupt transfer of the train of thought from one track to another,

> *... the emotive change which the narrative carried cannot be so transferred owing to its greater inertia and persistence; discarded by reason, the tension finds its outlet in laughter.*[7]

The pun is a good example of what Koestler regards as bisociation, for in the pun we perceive two strains of thought, in this case conencted by an acoustical knot of two similar sounds. Bisociation can be perceived in the Disney characters where there is an intersection between man and animal; in impersonation as the impersonator is two people at one time; in parody which is the intersection of the trivial and the exalted; as well as in caricature and satire. Thus,

> *the bisociative shock shatters the frame of complacent habits of thinking, the seemingly obvious is made to yield its secret.*[8]

The humorist joins two normally incompatible matrices together and,

> *His audience . . . has its expectations shattered and its reason affronted by the impact of the second matrix on the first; instead of fissure there is collision, and in the mental disarray which ensues, emotion, deserted by reason, is flushed out in laughter.*[9]

Sigmund Freud was particularly interested in jokes, their relation to the unconscious, and their similarity to dreams, the main distinguishing factor between the two being that dreams are oriented towards the individual while jokes are oriented towards the social. The essence of the joke, like that of dreams, lies in brevity, although brevity in itself is not necessarily comic. It has to be a brevity of a particular kind, what Freud refers to as "joke brevity." In studying a great number of jokes, Freud was able to discern various techniques used in jokes (double entendre, condensation, modification, allusion); however, "All these techniques are dominated by a tendency to compression, or rather to saving. It seems to be a question of economy."[10]

Freud's insight into the purpose of jokes has more to do with our project than his interest in the technique of jokes. Freud divided the purpose of jokes into two categories, that of non-tendentious (innocent) jokes and tendentious jokes. By tendentious Freud meant jokes that have an aggressive, insulting, hostile, or wounding purpose behind them. This generally requires at least a third person to be present for the derived pleasure to be fully enjoyed. Tendentious jokes rise from areas where there are social restrictions and repressions (e.g. anger, sexuality). For instance,

> *A joke will allow us to exploit something ridiculous in our enemy which we would not, on account of obstacles in our way, bring forward openly or consciously; once again, then, the joke will evade restrictions and open sources of pleasure that have become inaccesible.*[11]

A certain pleasure is derived from this pursuit. In the case of a non-tendentious joke the pleasure lies in the enjoyment of the joke alone and not its scoring off an enemy. It is in this area that we will take a theological interest linking tendentious humor and sin. It should be noted that, according to Freud, even non-tendentious or innocent jokes can conceal an ulterior motive,

> *The motive force for the production of innocent jokes is not infrequently an ambitious urge to show one's cleverness, to display oneself — an instinct that may be equated with exhibitionism in the sexual field.*[12]

In a Freduian understanding, the joke may often be Janus-like in character; the one face presenting a socially acceptable side, while the other face looks toward less acceptable, unconscious and not so moral motives. On occasion a joke can be " . . . a double-dealing rascal who serves two masters at once."[13]

Freud places jokes, the comic, and humor in different categories. Two useful insights of Freud concerning the category of humor will be used in this project. The first is Freud's reference to humor as a means of unmasking. Truth is sometimes concealed by an act of deception. Parody and travesty, particularly, serve in the role of unmasking. Humor has a significant role to play in revealing truth to us as Freud notes,

> *The unmasking is equivalent here to admonition; such and such a person, who is admired as a demi-god, is after all only human like you and me.*[14]

The way in which this takes place is of our concern, for unmasking can be cruel and insensitive in its undertaking as well as charitable and prudent.

The second interest to the project is Freud's concept of "the economy of pity." By this he means the role of humor in adversity and suffering as a means of defusing the situation of some of its negativity.

> ... *the humor that smiles through tears. It withdraws part of its energy from the affect and in exchange gives it a tinge of humor.*[15]

In so doing, humor is a defensive process that transforms into pleasure, by the discharge of laughter, some of the unpleasantness of the situation. This seems to be akin with Jesus' teaching that one can rejoice and be glad even in times of persecution (Matthew 5:12).

Freud clearly perceives that humor is linked to very deep, personal, and unconscious forces within the personality which must surely challenge the Christian to conscientiously and continually examine and refelct on his/her use of humor and call the church community as a whole to the responsible, charitable and mature employment of humor and the comic spirit within the household of faith as well as without in her witness and mission.

Upon learning that the focus of this professional project would be in the area of the presence and function of humor in a religious community, and the training of a team to utilize humor as a form of ministry, many persons immediately assumed that this project had to do with religious jokes. While religious jokes are not necessarily excluded from this project, the joke being a legitimate and recognized form of humor, this is certainly not the prime interest of this project. A much broader range of humor will be embraced ranging from parody to puns, from sarcasm to satire, from irony to comic exaggeration, wit, quips, and repartee. The average reader may not be aware that there are as many as 27 recognized forms of humor and more may be added to that list. A partial list of the forms of humor is included in the Appendix (Appendix C).

Humor and the comic spirit is an integral part of our human nature. It is a valuable gift bestowed upon us by God in the *imago Dei*. We recognize both the comic in ourselves and the comic in our culture. It is one of the qualities and gifts that sets us apart from the animals that distinguishes man as *homo risens*, the laughing creature. Humor is part of the make-up of our society, indeed it seems that laughter has a basic need to be shared in order to be fully enjoyed. Comedy and irony make a substantial contribution to our theater and entertainment. Humor also pervades our church communities and fellowships, and it is difficult to conceive of a Christian group in which the presence of humor is totally excluded. Even the hymnist invites us to worship God with a touch of mirth;

> *All people that on earth do dwell,*
> *Sing to the Lord with cheerful voice.*
> *Him serve with mirth, his praise forth tell*
> *Come ye before him and rejoice.*[16]

It is regrettable that while laughter is frequently enjoyed among the members of a church community, there is a hesitancy in linking humor to the Scriptures, and especially to the teachings of Jesus. Many are uneasy and reluctant to welcome laughter into the sanctuary and the worship service. There are a number of factors that have contributed to this state of affairs, including Catholic asceticism; an austere Protestant puritan heritage; a 19th century legacy emphasising the divine wrath and judgment; the focus of the faith on the agony, suffering, passion, death, and crucifixion of Jesus; and the problems encountered in multi-translations (from Aramaic to Greek to Latin to King James' English). Peculiar to humor in the Scripture is the recognized fact that body language, an important part of all communication, and essential to humor, cannot be transcribed, thus rendering many portions of Scripture flat and literal. This unfortunate accretion of factors that has all but stifled the comic spirit in the Scripture and worship is gradually being lifted as an increasing number of studies are revealing the original presence of humor in these areas and awakening a fresh interest and acceptance within the Christian community. Part of the intent of this professional project will be to address this issue, and to seek to introduce a scriptual and theological perspective on humor and to expand the function of humor to include ministry and service in a local congregtion.

ENDNOTES

[1] Henri Bergson, *An Essay on Comedy* ed. Wylie Sypher (New York: Doubleday Anchor Books, 1956), p. 74.

[2] Ibid., p. 79.

[3] Ibid., p. 81.

[4] Ibid., p. 90.

[5] Ibid., p. 97.

[6] Arthur Koestler, *The Act of Creation* (New York: The MacMillan Company, 1964), p. 35.

[7] Ibid., p. 59.

[8] Ibid., p. 73.

[9] Ibid., p. 94.

[10] Sigmund Freud, *Jokes and their Relation to the Unconscious* (New York: W.W. Norton & Company, 1963), p. 42.

[11] Ibid., p. 103.

[12] Ibid., p. 143.

[13] Ibid., p. 155.

[14] Ibid., p. 202.

[15] Ibid., p. 232.

[16] All People That on Earth Do Dwell — attr. to William Kethe. *The Methodist Hymnal* (Nashville: The Abingdon Press, 1964), Hymn No. 21.

Chapter 1
HUMOR IN THE SCRIPTURE

The collection of the holy books that comprise the canons of the Old and New Testament Scripture are not normally viewed as having too much in common with the subject of humor. Laughter and humor often appear to be sacrilegious, profane, and even to ridicule religious values. The New Testament nowhere mentions that Jesus ever laughed, though it says that he wept (John 11:35). In a culture in which laughter often ridicules and trivializes, it is understandable that many would wish to exclude it from the sacred. For some, mirth and religious faith are mutually exclusive. Reinhold Niehbur has written that laughter is acceptable,

> ... *in the vestibule of the Temple, the echo of laughter in the temple itself, but only faith and prayer and no laughter, in the holy of holies.*[1].

When it comes to the Scriptures, there are a number of reasons as to why the presence of humor is not easily recognized. First, there is the problem presented by literalism. Humor is contingent on the way language is employed, the common knowledge of the prevailing culture, the use of body language in communicating the comic intention, and signals and clues provided by the speaker indicating that what he/she says is to be taken ambiguously. None of the above translate easily into the written word. Inflection, body movement, and other allusions on which the comic spirit is dependent are left behind when the oral is transcribed and is unable to carry the intent of meaning from the spoken word to the written word:

> *Literalism narrows meaning to exactly what is said and flattens it to surface dimensions. As it tries to take a joke*

> *literally, the subtle nuances, the double meanings, the play-on words — above all — the humor gets lost.*[2]

And again:

> *Face to face verbal irony is usually not difficult to decipher. The ironic speaker may wink or smile, exaggerate her tone or quite subtly modify her manner in countless ways in order to signal us that her words do not themselves speak the whole truth. The strictures of writing, however, do not permit such immediate indication.*[3]

For instance, a play-on word phrase in the Aramaic language which would be comic to the listeners at the time, when translated into Greek, then into Latin, and then into the King James English (and read from the pulpit in a parsonic tone two thousand years later), almost entirely loses the original impact and significance of the pun. Recent research has been able to retrieve many of these playful nuances that have been "lost" in the translation. A good example of the recovery of the presence of puns in the Scripture is in Moffat's translation of Samson's victory cry where such a play on words becomes evident:

> *With the jaw-bone of an* **ass**
> *I plied them in a m***ass**!
> *With the jaw-bone of an* **ass**
> *I have* **ass**sailed **ass**ailants!
> >   Judges 15:16

One suspects that there are many other passages that are waiting to be liberated by literary research, which in turn will lead us to a deeper appreciation of the humorous side of the Scriptures:

> *Comic devices are by no means foreign to the Bible. They are not always easy to see because of the enormous*

> *problems in trying to translate puns, play on words, ironic twists, satirical allusions. We usually miss the punch line and the point as well. As we say, it loses something in translation. Humorous expressions and the contexts that make them humorous are the most difficult items to convey from one language to another, even with cumbersome footnotes or parenthetical explanations and once explained, they cease to be humorous anyway.*[4]

Hence we recognize that much of the original humorous and comic intent of prophet, psalmist, sage, evangelist, and apostle has been lost in the course of transition from one language and culture to another.

Second, the focus of the Christian proclamation on the salvific and efficacious work of Christ eclipses the presence of humor in the scripture and in the life and ministry of Jesus. The proclamation of Christ's passion and death introduces a seriousness and reverence which tends to preempt all else in his life and ministry. The evangelists devote more interest to the passion, suffering, agony, and crucifixion of Jesus than to the rest of his ministry. St. John condenses three years of ministry into the first 11 chapters of his gospel account, and then devotes the remaining 10 chapters to just one week, the last week of Christ's life. It is not likely that anyone of the Christian faith would wish to reduce this reverence in any way, or seek to replace it with a focus on Christ's humor; it is simply pointed out that the focus on the salvific work of Christ tends to obscure other areas of Christ's person and work which legitimately exist in their own right and proper place. The comic playfulness of Jesus, particularly in his teachings, is one of the areas that is affected. Hussey, writing about the effect that somberness has in eclipsing the humor of Jesus says:

> *Unhappily, however, the solemn Hebraic deification and the lacrimose sentimentalization of His life have almost totally obscured His humor.*[5]

A third factor that detracts from the easy recognition of humor in the scripture is that of the dubious legacy our century has received from the almost stifling interest that the last century showed in the divine wrath and judgment. Many preachers of that era felt it necessary to dangle their listeners over the flames of a burning hell. While the intent may have been to drive souls into the kingdom of heaven, the side effect was to drive all notions of humor out of the Bible and religion itself. It is unfortunate that such a powerful and persuasive force has continued to work its effect into the early and mid 20th century.

Acknowledging the eclipsing effects that literalism, the focus on the passion of Christ and his cross, and the legacy of the last century have in drawing attention away from any humor that might be present in the Scriptures, we may begin to search for the presence of the comic spirit and liberate it from its bonds. Humor is a God-given and spiritual gift which is good; it appears to be universal; and it is reasonable to anticipate its presence in holy writings as anywhere else. Over the past two decades, more and more scholars have given serious attention to seeking out the presence and function of humor in the Old and New Testaments and particularly in the life and ministry of Jesus.

HUMOR IN THE OLD TESTAMENT

There are, of course, a number of passages in the Old Testament that will be instantly recognized as having a humorous vein. Noah and his ark of animals has been the source of inspiration for the comic spirit and has provided perennial delight for adults and children alike. So, for the matter, has Jonah and the Whale, the whole book evidencing comic satire at its scriptural best. Beyond those obvious passages, a careful study of the Old Testament will reveal the presence of humor in many other parts such as the Torah, the history, psalms, and the prophets.

The Torah

The *locus classicus* for the presence of laughter in the Scripture is in Genesis 21:6, where Sarah, the wife of Abraham, upon giving birth to a male child in her extreme old age and thus bringing Abraham the much desired heir, announces, "God has made me to laugh so that all who hear shall laugh with me." This incident serves to draw attention to God as the initiator of laughter and the presence of the comic spirit in the divine plan. The child that is born to Abraham and Sarah is named Isaac (Yitschaq), which means the "son of laughter." Here in the holiest of the holy books, the books of Moses, the Torah, and adjacent to the law itself, is the comic spirit. At the very inception of the chosen race from which the Messiah will be born and the salvation of the world ushered in, we discover the presence of laughter. Israel, the convenant community, is born in laughter, a foretaste of the great joy yet to be revealed in Jesus.

History and Psalms

There are many examples of humor in Old Testament history and the psalms. One of the better known incidents is that of Yahweh addressing the "brave" Gideon hiding in a winepress with the words, "You mighty man of valour," (Judges 6:12), while in Esther there is the comic irony of Hanan eagerly building the gallows for Mordecai, oblivious to the fact that they will be used for his own execution (Esther 5:14).

The psalms are filled with references to God laughing in the heavens (Psalms 2:4) and at the feeble attempts of those who go against his purposes (Psalms 59:8). One of the most interesting texts, however, is about the sheer delight that God takes in playing with his creatures, particularly Leviathan who sometimes appears to be like a crocodile while at other times a kind of Loch Ness monster of the deep. Psalm 104:26 says,

"There ships move about with Leviathan, which you formed to make sport of it"; and in Job 41:5 God asks the bewildered complainant if he (Job) is able to play with Leviathan — the inference being that God does! While the ascription of laughter to God may at times be a crude anthropomorphism, it is nonetheless indicative of the fact that the early Hebrew mind perceived humor, laughter, and the comic spirit in the divine nature.

The Prophets

Deutro-Isaiah reveals a subtle humor as he proclaims against the folly of idol worship in his story of the man who cuts a tree in half and uses one half for firewood while the other half he makes into an idol for worship:

> *And after his care, he uses part of the wood to make a fire to warm himself and bake his bread and then — he really does — he takes the rest of it and makes himself a god — a god for men to worship.*
> *(Isaiah 44:15)*

Or again, railing at the sins of his people with biting sarcasm, "Woe to heroes — at drinking wine! valiant men — at mixing liquors!" (Isaiah 5:22)

The Book of Jonah, as Conrad Hyers has observed, is rightly understood as comic satire:

> *Throughout the book of Jonah, the devices used are the stock-in-trade of comedy: overstatement, understatement, surprise, opposite reaction, inconsistency, inappropriate response, ludicrous behavior, absurdity . . . our laughter at Jonah becomes a judgment on ourselves. In enjoying his wisdom turned into foolishness, we discover the foolishness of our own wisdom. This is the genius of great comedy, and the book of Jonah is one of the world's greatest and earliest comedies.*[6]

Amos, too, provides a comic perspective in the irony of the simple farmer standing before the King and the courts of Israel with the word of God.

Though not abounding in humor, the comic presence may often be detected in all the major writings of the Old Testament, the torah, the history, the psalms, and the prophets affirming that humor has its place among the holy books.

Jakob Jonsson's book, *Humor and Irony in the New Testament, Illuminated by Parallels in the Talmud and Midrash*, draws attention to the use of rabbinic humor and prophetic irony that provides the Jewish roots of Christian humor. In an article reviewing Jonsson's work, *The Joyful Noiseletter* writes,

> *Jonsson observes that the Jewish rabbis, before and after Jesus, were aware that paradox, sympathetic irony and humor can be effective teaching methods. Jonsson found Jewish humor revealed in folk songs, parables and anecdotes and in the biting irony and satire of the prophets.*
>
> *"It also seems to have been very common among the rabbis to start their discourse by saying something humorous in order to cheer their students," Jonsson noted. "The Hebrews do not seem to have been afraid of dealing humorously with the Scriptures . . . the rabbis objected only when the Bible was parodied disrespectfully or used to express improper ideas."*
>
> *This helps us to a better understanding of how the Rabbi Jesus taught, says Jonsson. Jesus, he insists, also used humour (sic) to teach.*[7]

HUMOR IN THE NEW TESTAMENT

The Life and Teaching of Jesus

L.M. Hussey, one of the pioneers in the area of humor in the life and ministry of Jesus, argues that the humor of

Christ can be detected more clearly in the synoptic gospels than in John's gospel; and even in the synoptic gospels, the humor of Jesus reveals itself more by contrast to the author's intent than by the writer himself.

> *Set against the solemn, humorless narrative of the gospel author are the literally repeated words of Jesus, and often they are quite out of key with the gospel author's sobrieties.*[8]

Hussey also ascribes to the point of view that all the humanity has been "squeezed out of Jesus" by well-meaning but abysmally serious-minded redactors.

Jesus' teachings appear to be rich in a variety of humorous techniques such as comic exaggeration, comic reversals, paradoxes, and irony.

Irony

There are many good examples in the synoptic gospels, particularly Matthew, of Jesus' adept use of irony, for instance in his references to:
- "the blind leading the blind so that both fall into the pit" (Matthew 15:14);
- "thistles growing on fig trees" (Matthew 7:16);
- "whitewashing the outside of the sepulchre" (Matthew 23:27);
- "garnishing the tombs of the prophets their fathers have killed" (Matthew 23:29).

Irony arises from the mind's keen awareness of incongruities in people's lives. Jesus was keenly aware of these spiritual contradictions, particularly in the myopic and serious attitude of the scribes and Pharisees, and was quick to point them out. Presumably not funny to the recalcitrant those who were able to see the irony of their actions and laugh at themselves were in a position for new growth.

Comic Exaggeration and Hyperbole

Comic exaggeration deals with one of the most delightful areas of Jesus' humor. It tends to be less polemical and more epistemological in its intent. Good examples of his use of this form of humor are:
- "the camel passing through the eye of the needle" (Matthew 19:24);
- "the filtering of the gnat only to swallow the camel" (Matthew 23:24);
- "the washing of the outisde of the cup only to drink from the dirty inside" (Matthew 23:25);
- "the blind leading the blind into a ditch" (Matthew 15:14);
- "the splinter in the one eye and the log in the other" (Matthew 7:34);
- the discrepancy between the loans of two debtors (Matthew 18:28);
- letting the dead bury the dead (Matthew 8:22).

Jesus appeared to enjoy this form of teaching and it is a true expression of his own comic view of life. No wonder "the common people heard him gladly" (Mark 12:37), and "his teaching was not like that of the scribes and pharisees" (Matthew 7:29). Jesus' irony still speaks to the scribe and Pharisee that abides within the well meaning disciple of today.

Comic Reversals

Comic reversals are particularly noticeable in Christ's parables in which the listeners would be surprised and delighted as the story reversed the fortunes and status of the characters. In the use of comic reversal the normally accepted order in society is changed and the listeners invited to imagine the comic situations as the top becomes the bottom, the common exalted, and the last made first. Good examples of these humorous teachings of Christ are evident in:

- The Good Samaritan (Luke 10:30);
- The rich man and Lazarus (Luke 16:19);
- The Pharisee and the Publican (Luke 18:9);
- The Great Supper (Luke 14:15).

Note, also, how Christ reverses the gift of the widow's two mites and the gifts of the rich. The theme appears in "The Magnificat," where Mary foresees that her son will be the cause of many reversals, "The mighty brought low and the poor exalted, the rich sent empty away and the poor filled with good things" (Luke 1:46). The comic reversals become a form of comic justice.

Paradoxes

Paradoxes have a humorous quality about them, often delighting the hearer by the seemingly baffling presentation of the truth and their reversal of the generally accepted norm. Paradoxes were very much a part of the teaching of Jesus:

- "But many that are first shall be last; and the last shall be first" (Matthew 19:30);
- "He that finds his life shall lose it; and he that loses his life for my sake shall find it" (Matthew 10:39);
- "He that is greatest among you, let him be the younger; and he that is chief, as he that doth serve" (Luke 22:26).

Consider also many of the Beatitudes of Jesus in Matthew, Chapter 5, such as "the meek shall inherit the earth," and "blessed are those that mourn." Humor, as we have noted, is concerned with life's incongruities and contradictions. Life is often complex and its apparent contradictions are explored in the paradox:

> *Christ's use of the paradox was appreciated by the perceptive, it was missed by the unhumorous and literal*

> minded . . . the entire process of finding similarity in apparent difference, which makes parable possible, is deeply paradoxical.[9]

In many ways, Jesus himself is the highest expression of paradox presenting the divine in human form. This truth is captured by the 17th century poet and hymnist, Richard Crashaw, in his "Hymn on the Holy Nativity."

> *Welcome, all wonders in one sight,*
>   *Eternity shut in a span,*
> *Summer in winter, day in night,*
>   *Heaven in earth, and God in man!*
> *Great little one! whose all-embracing birth*
> *Lifts earth to heaven, stoops heaven to earth.*[10]

Donald E. Messer, President of Illif School of Theology in Denver, Colorado, in a recent article, *The Good Shepherd: An Oxymoron?* suggests another possible form of humor used by Jesus in his teaching ministry, an oxymoron. An oxymoron is the juxtaposition of two seemingly contradictory terms as, for example, "the good Samaritan" would be. To listeners of the period "good" and "Samaritan" were mutually exclusive terms and the bringing together of these terms is as humorous as the modern equivalent of an "honest politician." Similarly, Messer reasons, was the juxtaposition of "good shepherd," for shepherds of the day were notoriously dishonest and known for their pilfering of the flocks.

> *The value of this type of speech is that it jars the readers to new awareness or startles the listener to new understandings. In the hands of an artist, an oxymoron like "thunderous silence" paints an unforgettable word portrait.*
>
> *Jesus was a communicator of ideas through the art of imaging par excellence. A metaphorical thinker, not a systematic theologian, Jesus knew the serendipitous art of creating the new by transforming the old. In daring*

> *fashion he would creatively appropriate the contradictory or unexpected and reverse religious understandings.*[11]

The humor of Jesus is seldom, if ever, flippant, nor does it seek to focus on humor as an end in itself; in most cases it seeks to be redemptive by being revealing, it is pedagogic and even mnemonic in its intent. Jesus wanted truth to be remembered and employed one of the basic and most positive ways of doing that — the humorous and comic method. Steimle and Rice draw attention to the redemptive element in Christ's use of irony, "Ironic criticism arises to amend the incongruity, not to destroy or annihilate it."[12] Trueblood puts it more forcefully:

> *We seek humor for humor's sake. There seems to be little or none of this in the recorded words of Christ, where the purpose is always the revelation of some facet of truth which would not otherwise be revealed. The humor of Christ is employed, it would appear, only because it is a means of calling attention to what would, without it, remain hidden or unappreciated. Truth, and truth alone, is the end.*[13]

I tend to disagree with Trueblood that Jesus did not at times enjoy humor for humor's sake, but acknowledge that for the most part Jesus' use of humor was to make the truth explicit. It is well worth noting that Jesus saw the release from suffering and hardship in terms of being able to laugh once again. He announces that "Those who weep now shall laugh" (Luke 6:21).

Irony in the Fourth Gospel and Paul

John's gospel, while evidencing less of Christ's use of humor, carries its own form of humor, particularly that of irony. Indeed, Jesus appears as his own expression of the ironic as the carpenter from Galilee who confounds the learned scribes and Pharisees. The irony is implicit from the very first chapter where Nathaniel asks of Jesus, "Can any good thing come out of Nazareth?" (John 1:46).

> *The Gospel of John contains motifs which are highly ironical. Observe, for example the interesting interplay on the theme of the weak and the strong. Who gives the most direct witness to Christ? An outsider, a Samaritan woman. Who claims the body of Christ after crucifixion? The strong disciples? No, two weak ones — Nicodemus, who comes off quite badly earlier in the Gospel, and Joseph of Arimathea. Who is the indisputable Victor in the Gospel? The man crucified. All are examples of an ironical treatment of a major motif in the Gospel of John.*[14]

The Pauline epistles are filled with irony, especially first Corinthians. The Apostle himself is aware of the irony of his own ministry, "And last of all, as one born out of due time, he appeared to me also. For I am the least of the apostles, that am not meet to be called an apostle, because I persecuted the church of God" (1 Corinthians 15:8-9). It is the least of the Apostles that gives us the majority of our New Testament! Again it is the one who is, "prisoner of Jesus Christ" (Philipines 1:1) who brings the message of "freedom from sin . . . freedom from righteousness . . . freedom from law . . . freedom from death" (Romans 6:18,20, 7:3, 8:2). Paul fears that the ultimate irony of preaching the Gospel could be that, "after I have preached to others, I myself should be rejected" (1 Corinthians 9:27). One other example from Corinthians is the irony of the gospel before the world for, "God chose the foolish things of this world that he might shame them that are wise; and God chose the weak things of the world, tht he might put to shame the things that are strong; and the base things of the world that are despised, did God chose, yea and the things are are not, that he might bring to nought the things that are" (1 Corinthians 1:27-28).

The biblical sense of humor is surely an echo of the divine sense of humor and delight in created life. Not only is there humor in the Bible but humor itself is biblical. Let us not be too easily disarmed by the presence of humor in the Old and New Testament scriptures. Humor is a subtle weapon, a two-edged sword that cuts through many defenses and makes the heart vulnerable to its good intent — the word of God. W. R. Mueller refers to the special ability of the comic:

> *Biblical comedy exposes men's weaknesses and follies, but always with compassion; it makes clear the wide gap between the human and the divine, sometimes arousing its protagonists from apathy, sometimes purging incipient builders of Babellian towers of the pride that kills.*[15]

Bob Parrot makes a significant link between humor and scripture:

> *A playful sense of humor is the key to unlocking some of the mysteries of the Bible. We dare not laugh at Scripture as if it were funny. The book remains God's revelation to us! But we can laugh at ourselves in others, in the Bible. The book remains sacred because it is God's book. Yet it contains humorous episodes because our incongruities in others are in it.*[16]

ENDNOTES

[1] Reinhold Neihbur, *Discerning the Signs of the Times: Sermons for Today and Tomorrow*, (London: SCM Press, 1946):115.

[2] Conrad Hyers, *And God Created Laughter* (Atlanta: John Knox Press, 1987), p. 3.

[3] Paul Duke, *Irony in the Fourth Gospel* (Atlanta: John Knox Press, 1985), p. 32.

[4] Hyers, p. 3.

[5] L.M. Hussey, "The Wit of the Carpenter," The *American Mercury* V (July 1925):336.

[6] Hyers, p. 96.

[7] *The Joyful Noiseletter*, Vol. 3 No. 1 (Jan-Feb. 1988):1.

[8] *Hussey*, p. 329.

[9] Elton Trueblood, *The Humor of Christ*, (New York: Harper and Row, 1975), p. 43.

[10] *The Oxford Book of Carols*, (London: Oxford University Press, 1964), Hymn No. 124.

[11] Donald E. Messer, *Circuit Rider*, Vol. 11 No. 11 (Jan. 1988):4.

[12] Edmund Steimle, Morris Niedenthal, and Charles Rice, *Preaching the Story*, (Philadelphia: Fortress Press, 1983), p. 143.

[13] Trueblood, p. 52.

[14] Duke, p. 7.

[15] W. R. Mueller, "God's Fools: Biblical and Modern," *Theology Today* 23 (Jan. 1967):543.

[16] Bob Parrot, "Ontology of Humor: A Basis for Biblical Exegesis," *Perkins Journal* 32 (Fall 1978):28.

Chapter 2
HUMOR AND THEOLOGY

Thomas Oden, in both the introduction and postscript to his first volume of systematic theology, *The Living God*, affirms the significance of the theo-comic for theology:

> *Because of piety's penchant for taking itself too seriously, theology more than the literary, humanistic, and scientific studies — does well to nurture a modest, unguarded sense of comedy. Some comic sensibility is required to keep in due proportion the pompous pretentions of the study of divinity.*[1]

Humor and theology, although distinct disciplines, at times share a common interest. Both are concerned about life's incongruities, the gap between the exalted and the humble, the poor and the rich, the wise and the foolish, and the human trying to be divine, seeking to redress these discrepancies in their own way. The comic spirit expression in its many forms delights to portray such reversals; and theology, reflecting on the witness of scripture, anticipates such reversals from the divine action in the human arena, as for example those predicted in the Magnificat (Luke 1:46). Even as the prophets of the Old Testament pointed out to their community of faith that which was contradictory between the covenant and their actions, so also humor can, in its own way, draw attention to our incongruities that illustrate the discrepancy between our profession and our practice, our creed and our conduct. There is no intention to suggest that humor on its own has the same potency as the prophetic "Thus saith the Lord . . .," merely to draw attention to the fact that on occasion the prophet may employ the comic tools, particularly irony, for the prophetic purpose, and theology need not, indeed ought not, be devoid of humor in order to be effective. In this section we shall consider the major categories of theology and the presence of humor in each category.

HUMOR AND THE CREATOR

The laughter of God is well attested to in Scripture, which fact is, regrettably, frequently ignored in favor of attributing the more austere qualities to the divine nature. In the Book of Psalms it says, "He that sitteth in the heavens shall laugh," (Psalm 2:4); "He [God] shall laugh at him," (Psalm 37:13); "Thou shalt laugh at them" (Psalm 59:8); and in the Book of Job, "God fills our mouths with laughter" (Job 8:21). While many verses certainly attribute laughter to the divine nature, the context is sometimes of a negative form of laughter, that of scorn or derision. From our perspective, this may seem to be an unworthy attribute for God. Yet, however crude the anthropomorphism may be, it is nonetheless indicative of an early notion of God having a sense of humor and the ability to delight in the foibles of men as they attempt to assert their wills against his divine purpose. Even poor laughter is contingent on the ability to be able to laugh in the first instance. The inference is legitimate; if there is room for one kind of laughter, that presupposes room for another kind, that of the good and wholesome laughter. The notion is probably correct; however, the anthropomorphism needs to be refined.

HUMOR IN THE CREATION

If there is humor in the divine nature, then it would be reasonable to expect that this quality would express itself in the creation and the creatures. It is a most natural thing for people to find mirth in looking upon the animals and amusement in the created realm. Life appears everywhere to be filled with this comic spirit; the antics of monkeys and their close companion the orangutan; the spouting whale; the whiskers of the sea lion; the laughing hyena; the trunk of the elephant; the cheeks of the chipmunk; from "green alligators and long necked geese, to humpty back camels and chimpanzees." Even the "creepy crawlies" evidence the comic among some of their members. Psalm 104:6 and Job 41:5 refer to God sporting with Leviathan whom He seems to have made for the sheer delight of such a creature. Man seeking his own humorous entertainment invariably turns to the animals. Consider the most popular cartoons featuring Daffy Duck, Mickey Mouse, Yogi Bear, Pluto, Snoopy, Chip 'n Dale and others too numerous to mention. It is an unfortunate matter that laughter has been neglected in the creation stories of Genesis.

THE IMAGO DEI

The highest act of creation is a reflection of the divine, "So God created man in his own image, in the image of God created he him; male and female created he them" (Genesis 1:27). It is humor, among the other spiritual gifts to man in the *imago Dei*, that sets man apart from the rest of creation and enables us to enjoy what the rest of creation cannot. It is difficult to conceive of the Creator bestowing such a gift as humor upon man while failing to enjoy the dimensions of the gift within the divine Self. Simple syllogistic logic affirms that you cannot have in the conclusion that which is not in the premise. Far more acceptable is the affirmation that because humor is first in the Divine, so also is it given as a gift to man in the *imago Dei*. It is the Torah, Genesis 21.6, that we have a direct statement that God has given the ability to laugh to men and women, "God has made me to laugh so that all who hear shall laugh with me" (Genesis 21:6).

HUMOR AND THE FALL

Humor, like all spiritual gifts, is subject to misuse, abuse, and to the corruption of its good intent. It is vulnerable to our sin. This is most evident in that which we commonly call "sick jokes" aimed at hurting, embarrassing, and excluding, and is found in such perverted forms of humor as ridicule, derision, sarcasm, mockery, and scorn:

> *Fallen laughter is the kind we employ when we wish to ridicule someone or elevate ourselves above others. It is what racists jokes and sexist jokes and Polish jokes are made of. We laugh at and not with others. And at its worst, fallen laughter can be malicious, cruel, sarcastic, mocking, arrogant, vulgar, bitter, and insane. The laughter of the crowd at Jesus' crucifixion was of this sort.*[2]

Laughter, as such, seeks to be exclusive rather than inclusive and separates, hurts, and injures the other. It is an injustice against the other, thus becoming a travesty of the command to love one's neighbor as oneself. Paul Homer decribes the low level to which humor can descend:

> *There is, too, that sickly humor which men enjoy because their own lives are mistaken and seldom serious. The man who postures, slobbers and drools, who indulges in depravity, ignorance, drunkenness, irresponsibility and finds that there are always those who will laugh, this man probably uses humor to keep the rendezvous with his own meaningless life. This is to laugh but almost without knowing why and being unable to afford the insight to find out. Men do use humor as a kind of shield, protecting themselves from anything which might reveal the ugly puddle inside.*[3]

Joel Goodman has set out a useful table comparing the positive and negative aspects of humor:

Laughing with	**Laughing at**
1. Going for the jocular vein.	1. Going for the jugular vein.
2. Based on caring.	2. Based on contempt.
3. Builds confidence.	3. Destroys confidence through putdowns.
4. Involves people in fun.	4. Excludes some people.
5. A person makes a choice to be butt of joke and laughs at himself.	5. A person has no choice in being made the butt of the joke.
6. Amusing — invites people to laugh.	6. Abusive — offends people.
7. Supportive.	7. Derogatory.
8. Brings people closer.	8. Divides people.
9. Leads to positive repartee.	9. Leads to putting down cycle.
10. Pokes fun at universal foibles.	10. Reinforces stereotypes by singling out a particular group as the butt.[4]

It is from the misuse, abuse, and corruption of the God-given quality of humor and laughter that one also needs redemption, for sin has tainted all human qualities including that of humor. It has even in this area set him in a bondage from which he needs to be liberated.

For some theologians, sin lies not so much in the corruption of humor but rather in its absence. It is in the repression of laughter and in taking ourselves too seriously, believing ourselves to be gods, where sin resides. It is in failing to laugh at ourselves that is the root of such sin. It is in arrogant seriousness that sin dwells. Hyers writes:

> *Without humor we become something less, not more, than human. We become not more divine but more demonic.*[5]

The fall into sin may be viewed, then, as a reduction of humor,

> *The fall of Adam was a fall into seriousness. And we have taken ourselves, our circumstances, our achievements, and our beliefs quiet seriously ever since.*[6]

This concept is well presented in Ken Kesey's, *One Flew Over the Cuckoo's Nest,* when Patrick McMurphy says, of the asylum,

> *"That's the first thing that got me about this place, there wasn't anybody laughing. I haven't heard a real laugh since I came through that door. . . . Man, when you lose your laugh you lose your footing."*[7]

Dante Alighieri in his *Divine Comedy* carries a similar idea of hell and purgatory being devoid of laughter but upon approaching the celestial sphere the sounds of the laughter of the universe fell upon his ears.

HUMOR AND REDEMPTION

Truth and Repentance

Present in one form or another in all humor is a degree of truth. The old adage, "Many a true word is spoken in jest," perceived this occurrence and drew attention to it. Most humor is based on incongruity, which in turn pre-supposes a perception of the congruous. Truth is the congruous quality that elicits incongruities. To encounter the truth is to have the opportunity for change (metanoia). Jesus taught that it is ". . . the truth that sets us free [from sin]" (John 8:32), and the acceptance of truth is a prerequisite for salvation.

In this respect humor can have a revelatory function inviting the recipient to embrace a new level of truth in his or her life. Bob Parrot expresses this notion in existentialist categories when he suggests that the truth in humor is able to reveal to us the gap between our estranged selves and our authentic selves.[8] In this revelatory moment, repentance and change becomes possible, humor affording us the opportunity to transcend ourselves for the moment. Truth in the form of humor is able to invite the fallen self to move away from incongruity and contradition and embrace a healthier refelction of the *imago Dei*. It ought to be noted that truth does not seek to resolve all contradictions in life, as if that were possible, but merely to resolve those conditions which result from sin being present in our actions and to redeem us from the corruption of our humor. It is accepted that even without sin men and women would still embrace the incongruous and contradictory in life but in a harmless fashion.

Forgiveness

The sin against the Holy Spirit (Matthew 12:31), also known as the "unforgivable sin," is generally understood to mean the sin of refusing to accept the forgiveness offered, rejecting the need to be forgiven, refusing ultimately to acknowledge one's sin and being unwilling to accept forgiveness, the inhibition being on the side of the sinner rather than a withdrawal of the offer from the divine side. When humor is able to lead us into the position of being able to laugh at ourselves, it allows forgiveness to take place. Laughing at ourselves is in some way a prerequisite for forgiveness. It is a self acknowledgement of our limits, foibles, and failures. Robert McAfee Brown perceives humor as redemptive insofar as it seeks to restore matters to a rightful perspective. Humor, when used with sensitivity and prudence, can be a great leveler, saving us from our grandiose ideas about ourselves and from the harm we can do from taking ourselves too seriously:

> *The saving grace of humor then, is not only in the ability to laugh, but (most savingly, most gracefully,) an ability to laugh at ourselves. It involves a willingness to be cut down to size and emerge liberated rather than devastated by the experience.*[9]

Humor can help us face our limitations as human beings and protect us from the ever present sin of seeking to conceive of ourselves in the central place that belongs to God. It is often only through the spectacles of humor that man is able to see himself as he is — that he is not the god he thought he was — and that God continues to love him despite his failures.

Furthermore, humor as a form of grace enables men and women to see the truth concerning themselves in a non-intimidating manner that does not destroy the ego and self esteem, but, on the contrary, brings a sense of laughter, release, well being and acceptance while it encourages and points toward the healing direction needed. Humor by its graceful and prudent way can lead not to despair but to redemption. It seeks to avoid embarrassment and hurt or the lowering of self-esteem, and with a comfortable recognition of life's contradiction brings our foibles before us with a sense of divine acceptance of ourselves despite our failures.

The comic spirit is often able to liberate the soul from isolation. Gary Davenport suggests that detachment and objectivity can result from laughter at oneself and is the first prerequisite for salvation; being social in its orientation, laughter begins to liberate us from the isolation our sin leads us into, a laughter that brings salvation from the prison of the self.[10]

> *Humility induces the ability to laugh at oneself and the refusal to take oneself altogether seriously. Laughter may open the way to love and forgiveness, for in laughter hostilities are softened, just as forgiveness allows former enemies to laugh together.*[11]

Humor is a redemptive work in us when it causes us to reevaluate our lives; it moves us from our innocence via the truth to compassion.

HUMOR AND COMPASSION IN CHRIST

Like most qualities, humor, too, has its reciprocal. As up correlates with down, inside to outside, good to evil, so humor correlates to compassion. The Book of Ecclesiastes places these two qualities side by side, "a time to weep and a time to laugh" (Ecclesiastes 3:4). The Book of Proverbs muses, "Even in laughter is the heart sorrowful" (Proverbs 14:13); and Jesus predicted that "Those who weep now shall laugh, while those who laugh now shall weep in time to come" (Luke 6:21).

Clinical psychologists have long perceived the intimate relation between compassion and humor; and it appears that the greater the capacity for the one quality, the greater the capacity for the other. Humor and compassion are linked proportionately. Certainly Jesus had deep compassion for the poor, the handicapped, the oppressed, the lame, the halt, and the blind as is evidenced by his healing ministry. If the intimate relation between compassion and humor is recognized, it would require us to anticipate the presence of humor in Jesus' nature and teaching ministry and to reflect on this theologically.

Soren Kierkegaard was keenly aware of the affinity between these two qualities. Lloyd Parrill writes:

> *At first glance, the comic and the tragic seem to have little in common, yet the humorist recognizes that they are essentially the same in that they are both based on the element of contradiction. The difference is that the tragic is characterized by hopelessness and despair, the comic by the hope it affords. Paradoxically, in the unity of the comic and the tragic, the humorist realizes that only by fully embracing the tragic element will healing occur whereas the comic apprehension once sufficed, now the humorist must look to the transcendence of faith, "humor is the last stage of existential inwardness before faith."*[12]

The first two actions of life are to cry and to gurgle, anticipating the range and relation of compassion and the comic spirit.

THE HUMAN NATURE OF CHRIST

Theologians from the early Christian centuries have jealously guarded the affirmation concerning the full human nature of Christ. Ever since Docetism reared its head, defenders of the faith have become the more adamant in affirming that Christ assumed a complete human nature in the incarnation. If human nature includes a sense of humor, which seems to be well nigh universal, it is inescapable that Jesus must have possessed this aspect of human nature as well and that on occasion he would initiate his own humorous perceptions on life, and in turn be amused by the humor he encountered in others. It would be difficult to maintain the full human nature of Christ if a sense of humor were to be excluded from him and would represent Christ as a kind of *tertium quid*, or demi-god. It is hard to conceive of a Savior devoid of a sense of humor or the ability to laugh, and one would wonder if that would be a salvation for us at all.

THE WORK OF THE HOLY SPIRIT

It is questionable as to whether the Holy Spirit could or would bestow a sense of humor upon some person. It would seem that such an activity would be a duplication of the gift already given to us in the *imago Dei*. The work of the Holy Spirit in regard to humor is more likely to be on the level of refining and cleansing. Given the misuse of this gift, the work of the Spirit would be to drive out of the soul that which spoils the gift and results in a toxic relation to the neighbor. As the Christian journeys towards wholesomeness, so also in this area the higher use and appreciation of the gift would evolve, removing all traces of scorn, derision, mockery, and sarcasm, and that which would offend the neighbor. Furthermore, the Spirit would quicken the good gift in the believer, enabling him to use it in love and charity. It needs to be reiterated that the work of the Holy Spirit is not to resolve all contradictions in human life and drive us into a merciless state of perfection, but to save us from presuming we are perfect and drive all sin out of our lives including the sin that corrupts or inhibits laughter. It is sin that is driven out, not necessarily the contradictions resulting from being both spirit and matter.

THE TRINITY

To be consistent within the Godhead, humor would have to evidence itself in God's three ways of being God — Creator, Son, and Holy Spirit. It is evident from the foregoing survey that the Creator laughs in the heavens, and reveals his humor in the created realm, especially in the same gift to man in the *imago Dei*; that Jesus embraces a full human nature which includes a sense of humor; and that this humor is present in his teachings and as the anticipated reciprocal of his great compassion; and the work of the Spirit is to refine the gift of humor, redeeming it from its fallen state and quickening it to its proper role in the believer's life. If the presence of humor could not be reasonably shown to be present in every part of the godhead, then its presence in one or another part would immediately be suspect. However, it has been reasonably shown that humor is present in all three persons of the godhead — Creator, Redeemer, and Spirit.

TOWARD A THEOLOGY OF HUMOR

From a scriptural presence and foundation, we have offered a reflection on the intersection of humor with some of the major areas of theological concern, that is, the Creator, creation, *imago Dei*, the fallen state of man, redemption, the nature of Christ, the work of the Spirit and its Trinitarian harmony.

Theology without the comic perspective can become destructive and harmful:

> *Religion, which has elevated the human spirit with visions of common bonds, self sacrifice, harmony, and compassion, has also proved to be one of the greatest single sources of segregation, pride, prejudice, antipathy, destruction, and bloodshed. Religious history is littered*

> *with reminders of the tragic possibilities of faith without humor and the sacred without the comic.*[13]

We need to keep the comic spirit in theology as a safety valve from our own seriousness, for a faith without humor can become a relentless form of unmerciful dogmatism. Besides, theology needs to reflect on the comic spirit as an integral part of human nature and seek to address the gospel to the joyous with men and women, not only address it to the negative condition:

> *It has recently been revealed that whereas we have a gospel for the alienated, the hurt, the depressed, the defeated, we have not a gospel for the well, the joyous, the busy, the engaged people of this world . . . it is more and more widely true that a gospel whose scope does not address people in their joyous, creative, constructive and effectual operations is unchallenging because uninteresting.*[14]

Conrad Hyers shares a similar perspective:

> *Unfortunately theologians and moralists had much to say about man's responsibility to work, but little about his responsibility to play; many words about seriousness and sobriety, few about nonsense and laughter . . . . Precious little has ever been said about humor as an aspect of the imago Dei, let alone as a dimension of the religious situation of the divine.*[15]

Even a theologian of the stature of Karl Barth, having completed a *Church Dogmatics* in twelve volumes, was able to realize in playful spirit how this monumentous work may be regarded by the angels:

> *The angels laugh at old Karl. They laugh at him because he tries to grasp the truth about God in a book of Dogmatics. They laugh at the fact that volume follows volume and each is thicker than the previous ones. As*

they laugh, they say to one another, "Look! Here he comes now with his little pushcart full of volumes of the Dogmatics!"[16]

ENDNOTES

[1] Thomas Oden, *The Living God*, (New York: Harper and Row, 1987), p. 1.

[2] Conrad Hyers, *And God Created Laughter*, (Atlanta: John Knox Press, 1987), p. 15.

[3] Paul Holmer, Something About What Makes It Funny, *Soundings* 57 (Summer 1974):167.

[4] Joel Goodman, "How to Get Smilage out of your Life," in Paul E. McGhee and Jeffery H. Goldstein, *Handbook of Humor Research*, (New York: Springer Verlag, 1983), p. 11.

[5] Conrad Hyers, *The Comic Vision and the Christian Faith*, (New York: The Pilgrim Press, 1981), p. 26.

[6] Hyers, p. 23.

[7] Ken Kessey, *One Flew Over the Cuckoo's Nest*, (New York: Viking Press/Penguin Books USA, 1962), p. 65.

[8] Bob W. Parrot, "Ontology of Humor: A Basis for Biblical Exegesis," *Perkins Journal* (Fall 1978):21.

[9] Robert McAfee Brown, "The Spirit's Eight Gifts," *Christianity and Crisis* 40 (Feb. 4, 1980):8.

[10] Gary Davenport, "Elliot's The Cocktail Party: Comic Perspective as Salvation," *Modern Drama* 17 (Summer 1974):303.

[11] Hyers, p. 49.

[12] Lloyd Parrill, "The Concept of Humor in the Pseudonymous Works of Soren Kierkegaard," *Drew Gateway*, Volume 46 (1976):116.

[13] Hyers, p. 51.

[14] W. H. Mullen, "Toward a Theology of Humor (with Response by Dr. Anderson)" *Christian Scholars Review* 3, No. 1 (1973):4.

[15] Conrad Hyers, "The Dialect of the Sacred and the Comic," *Cross Curents* (1969):72.

[16] *Portrait of Karl Barth*, trans. Robert McAfee Brown and George Casalis, (New York: Doubleday, 1963), p. 3.

Chapter 3

HUMOR IN THE SERVICE OF MINISTRY

Effective ministry in the church needs to be well grounded in Scripture and theological reflection. When securely rooted in these two areas, it most naturally flows out in service to others permeated with charity and goodwill. We have noted in the previous chapters that humor is amply present in the biblical witness and can sustain theological reflection in the major categories of theological discipline. There are many innovative, original, and effective ways in which humor is being used in the caring ministry of the church today. Although the ministries are often diverse, the common denominator is that of the prudent use of humor in the work and witness of the local congregation. In this section we shall explore several ways in which humor is being utilized in ministry.

HUMOR AND THE HEALING MINISTRY

Norman Cousin's book, *The Anatomy of an Illness*, was on the top of the New York Times Best Seller List when it was first published in the late 1970s. Suffering from a disease that caused him chronic pain and discomfort over a protracted period of time, Cousins fought back by seeking to mobilize his body's own healing resources. Working on the assumption that laughter could release a positive emotional force into his psyche and ease the pain in his body, Cousins hired a number of comedy films, such as Charlie Chaplain, the Marx Brothers, and Laurel and Hardy, and found that while watching these, his laughter seemed to significantly reduce his discomfort and pain. Cousins made a significant link between humor and healing and the therapeutic value of laughter.

The Institute for Advancement of Human Behavior, of which Cousins is a participant as adjunct Professor of Psychiatry and Behavioral Sciences of UCLA School of Medicine, has explored, expanded, and developed the therapeutic and healing role of humor, and the positive physical and emotional forces released by hearty laughter. At the fifth annual conference of the Institute held in Boston, Massachusetts in September, 1987, the theme for the conference was *The Power of Laughter and Play*, linking humor directly with health, creativity, the reduction of stress, and better living patterns. Titles of the lectures and workshops included, "Laugh Your Way to Health," "The Power of Humor in the Work Environment," "Humor and Health," and "Stress Management and Humor" (Appendix B).

There appears to be significant medical and psychological agreement that humor reduces stress, builds team feelings, raises the espirt de corps, defuses negative emotionally charged situations, helps reduce the likelihood of "burnout", and generally contributes to both better and longer living.

Jesus was concerned with healing and sought the well being of people not only in their physical state but also emotionally and spiritually. The church, seeking to emulate her Lord's compassion and desire to heal, does well to take cognizance of the significant contribution humor has to make to well being and health. This does not mean for the local congregation that one walks around with a repertoire of jokes, or that one attempts to make others laugh at every available opportunity. It could mean that our approach to spiritual health takes a preventive orientation insofar as learning not to take ourselves and our projects so seriously that we cannot allow ourselves the time to enjoy our work and "serve the Lord with mirth." A common snare of the religious life is that of taking our dogmas and projects so seriously that we become myopic and focus with such intensity on that which is before us that we block out all other perspectives. Jesus warned about the danger of over seriousness and taught that in religion one can begin "to look for the gnats while missing the camels" (Matthew 23:24).

This is not to say that we approach our church life with laxity, nor that we relinquish our enthusiasm or efforts, but rather with a spirit of lightheartedness and cheer, go about our work without overt seriousness or covert tension.

Furthermore, we may learn to discern incongruities in ourselves and in our congregation and come to accept our limitations. Sharing the contradictions we see in ourselves and our church life with prudence and sensitivity can help raise the esprit de corps, build team spirit, and promote wholesomeness and emotional and spiritual health in the community. Laughing with others and resolving not to laugh at others are part of health and healing in a community. Such an atmosphere, though seemingly ideal, is certainly balm to the wounded soul. The body is not a machine operated by the soul as *deux ex machina*, but sensitive spiritual tissue on which negative and positive emotions act, contributing to illness or well being. Laughter and humor have a significant contribution to make to health and wholeness.

HUMOR AND THE PREACHING MINISTRY

The worship service at any given church probably gathers more of the congregation in one place at one time than at any other church functions. In the worship service, at least in the Protestant tradition, a predominant amount of time is given to the proclaimed word, to preaching. It is in this area specifically, and in the liturgy generally, that the prudent use of humor has much to offer. The responsible use of humor from the pulpit can, in the first instance, help disarm the listeners of all kinds of defenses and negative "baggage" that they might be carrying, allowing the listener to become open and more receptive to the message of the day. Interspersed during the message, and related to its theme, humor can provide an "intellectual rest" along the way as the sermon journeys toward its goal, refreshing the listener. It can focus attention on the gospel, and enhance the fellowship of the congregation. It is apparent that Jesus used humor as he proclaimed the kingdom of God, using comic exaggeration, comic reversals, irony, and paradoxes, and that his teaching stood in contrast to the more serious and literal mindedness of the scribes and the Pharisees. Jesus was easier to listen to because of his prudent use of the comic, and "the crowds received him gladly" (Mark 12:37).

A more cynical perspective, yet not without a degree of truth, is that if you are going to tell people the truth, you had better make them laugh — else they will kill you. Certainly humor in the pulpit can provide a less intimidating way for people to be confronted with their incongruities, with a higher likelihood of their accepting the truth and working to resolve their life's contradictions.

Fred. B. Craddock, Professor of New Testament and Preaching at Candler School of Theology, teaches that humor is the honest reception of life's imagery and its use is sacred, profound, and significant and has a very definite place in the sanctuary. On the contrary, it is the altogether serious presentation of the gospel that can do the more harm:

> *This does not mean that he [preacher] tells jokes. Telling jokes is no clear sign of a sense of humor and is questionable pulpit practice with much common sense against it. But a sense of humor is simply the freedom to receive and to share life's imagery without the compulsion to evaporate the concrete into spiritual truths or melt it down into bland generalities. Thus understood humor becomes for the speaker and hearer a form of celebraiton, an expression of fellowship, a confession of trust in the Creator who made things as they are and who does not need the protection our humorless piety would afford.*[1]

Randall Nicholls makes an interesting point concerning the intimidating effect that the pulpit can have on the listener. The high pretensions, lofty ideals, moral injunctions, spiritual challenges, and awesome awareness of the divine flowing from the pulpit can be relentless and sometimes overpowering.

Nicholls illustrates his point with reference to attending a circus. In the presence of the super-talented performers, high wire walkers, acrobats, trapeze artists, the viewer is apt to begin to feel a sense of inadequacy and helplessness, a lack of self talent and inability. Then the clown appears between the acts and falls on his face, thus providing a comic relief from the intensity of the performance and also subtly restoring some of the audience's self-esteem. The clown serves to bring us back from the lofty world to the common bumblings of life. So too in worship and preaching, Nicholls suggests that the preacher be "sensitive," and "benevolent" to the fragility and limitations of his or her listeners:

> *When I listen to a preacher I want to know whether he or she conveys a sense of basic good will, of an awareness of my fragility, and of an ability to trim his or her faster movement, greater competence, and more knowing outlook, to allow me, the seasick passenger, to make the voyage without added trauma.*[2]

Truth without laughter can be extremely harsh, and it is love that presents its truth in the comic spirit. When the true comic spirit is in the preacher, it will flow naturally into the message and free him or her from artificial techniques that in the end tend to obscure rather than enhance the message. It is when the gospel message is forced into a straitjacket of seriousness and piety (into which it does not naturally or easily fit), or for that matter into an artificial comic structure, that the tone of the message becomes superficial and is not synchronized with life as it is recognized by the hearers:

> *Humor properly joined to the matter of the sermon, feels at home and is thus free to frolic, laugh, and celebrate the grace of God. Humor is, after all, inevitable in truly good preaching because all the right ingredients are present: concrete specific references, no one laughs at the general and abstract; . . . . Humor is, then, a genuine response to grace; grace works in us that most beautiful*

> *virtue, gratitude; and the grateful person acknowledges that there is usually a small party going on in the back of his mind. All this, of course, makes no sense to the humorless calculator who carefully inserts a joke here and there to break up the monotony of a sermon which, in its intense effort to be totally serious, generates smiles and muffled laughter.*[3]

An effective and caring ministry may be offered by the prudent use of humor from the pulpit, and laughter in the sanctuary and the comic spirit in the words of the liturgy serves to recognize rather than ignore one of the noble gifts of God to men and women.

HUMOR AND EDUCATION

Education at times can appear to be more of a task than an enjoyable pursuit, often compounded by peer group pressures and seemingly insurmountable material to absorb. While there are no shortcuts to a thorough education, humor can contribute to both the perception and retention of new knowledge. This process has sometimes been referred to as "comic epistemology."

Godspell, the Broadway stage production of the Gospel of Matthew, is an example of how the contents of an entire New Testament gospel may be encountered and largely remembered through a comic (yet serious) presentation of the life of Jesus. A fair percentage of the presentation concerned Jesus' teachings, particularly the Sermon on the Mount. In the medium of the comic spirit, it was easier for most people to receive, appreciate, and recall the teachings of Jesus than sitting down with a double columned small print King James' Version of the Bible and attempting to commit it to memory.

Another example of humor in the service of education is through the medium of animated Bible characters and stories. The Church School at Whitehouse United Methodist Church purchased a series of Old Testament stories animated by the well-known Hanna-Barbera company. These Old Testament stories were high quality production tapes coupled with biblical accuracy. Teachers report a marked increase in the attention span of the children while viewing Bible stories in this medium and a willingness to borrow the video films from the church library to take home to watch them again. There are some who are wary about using animation as a medium for teaching the Scriptures, suggesting a risk of reducing the message to the level of a Saturday morning cartoon show. However, there seems to be as great a risk in the more conventional mediums used for church school education, where the attention span is brief and church school is regarded as boring, with children "tuning out" and focusing their attention on other things. The eager acceptance of the stories in animated form is a "comic epistemology," as they encounter and learn the words of Scripture through animated characters. Comic illustration appears to achieve more when prudently applied (for example, Sesame Street) than "verbal prose" and as such serves as a mnemonic aid and tutor, improving perception, retention, and recall. Jospeh McLelland says:

> *Just as in classical drama the moment of recognition provides a shift in orientation, so the gospel story tells of a hidden God and the surprising joy he proves to be when recognized. This sort of cognition contributes to a kind of "comic espistemology" sadly missing from classical theism.*[4]

Humor often brings with it insight and understanding. It can illumine our self-understanding and bring truth concerning our world into focus. Its pedagogic role ought not to be underestimated.

HUMOR AND SPIRITUAL GROWTH

Spiritual growth is an elusive term to define, and difficult to measure or evaluate. It means one thing to one person, and something entirely different to another. Perhaps one aspect of spiritual growth may be encountered when a person is able to recognize an incongruity or contradiction in life and then take the appropriate action to resolve that contradiction, thus moving beyond it to a greater personal harmony. When this happens we may say that there has been personal and spiritual growth. The process, of course, repeats itself again and again. Humor adopts an almost prophetic role in relation to spiritual growth, pointing out both the contradiction and the congruity from which it diverges, making it possible for us to see where we ought to be. When that encounter with truth provided by humor is accepted and acted upon, a higher level of personal integrity results, giving rise to maturity and spiritual growth. This, obviously, is a difficult process to self initiate. There are a number of very gifted people who are able to provide these humorous yet truth-filled vignettes for us. Even as political cartoonists are able to present the contradictions of the political scene in the political cartoon (which helps the public and the politicians to see an issue that otherwise might be missed,) so also are there religious, ecclesiastical or theological cartoonists who are able to set before the church community some of her foibles, contradictions, and incongruities that might not be easily perceived in any other way. Two perceptive and ecclesiastically critical cartoonists are Doug Marlette (The Preacher) and Charles Schultz (Peanuts). Their syndicated cartoon strips provide us with much pertinent truth concerning the religious life. It may well be that the critical insights might come from cartoonists outside the church community who are able to see more of our shortcomings more objectively than we do ourselves. Cartoonists both inside and outside of the church may provide opportunity for spiritual growth by setting the truth in cartoon format. Not all cartoons necessarily provide for spiritual growth; some are simply funny situations, others are mere playfulness, still others are remarkably non-funny (except maybe to the cartoonist). It is a special kind of cartoon that contains the potential for spiritual growth and the opportunity for a shift in personal and spiritual orientation. It is such cartoons that serve as the social or religious conscience of the community in an iconoclastic or prophetic role. In the area of spiritual growth the ministry of humor always seeks to enrich, enhance, and inform life.

Humor, when employed in the service of ministry in Christ's name, needs to be accompanied with charity, prudence, insight, sensitivity, and care and as such can be the vehicle of potent spiritual energy to both the household of faith and those beyond who receive her message.

> *Those who are able to include themselves in their laughter are also able to include others in their generosity. A humor that heretofor has moved within the context of comic release and comic justice now moves within the context of empathy and kindred feeling. Humor is freed to become the humor of humility and compassion.*[5]

ENDNOTES

[1] Fred B. Craddock, *As One Without Authority*, (Nashville: Abingdon Press, 1986), p. 91.

[2] J. Randall Nicholls, *The Restoring Word*, (San Francisco: Harper and Row, 1987), p. 125.

[3] Fred B. Craddock, *Preaching*, (Nashville: Abingdon Press, 1985), p. 219.

[4] Joseph McLelland, "Doxology as Suspension of the Tragic," *Theology Today* 31 (July 1974):114.

[5] Conrad Hyers, *The Comic Vision and the Christian Faith*, (New York: The Pilgrim Press, 1981), p. 29.

Chapter 4
WORSHIP RESOURCES

There are numerous reasons why laughter and mirth are often minimized in the context of worship. Some of these reasons have been stated in the first part of this book. Briefly, the recorded word leaves behind context, body language, voice inflections, facial gestures, eye movements and other such signs that convey a message beyond the words themselves. Frequently, what began as humorous winds up as bland.

Second, the effects of an unfortunate legacy from the last century still lingers in many of our houses of worship. A morbid and threatening emphasis on hell, fire, and damnation was often employed to coerce people into the kingdom of God at the same time driving all mirth and frivoloty from their understanding of the Christian gospel and from the worship experience. This unfortunate dampening of the spirit reaches down and touches us today.

A third factor lies in central focus of the suffering, passion, and agony of Christ's sacrificial death. Time, place and season necessitate such an attitude of solemnity, but often this powerful proclamation unintentionally eclipses all other aspects of Jesus' humanity.

Last, Christian art, particularly middle age and renaissance, seldom depicts Jesus' countenance as being joyful or happy thus further compounding our overall impression of the lack of mirth and gaiety in his life. Today it is fitting that we seek to reclaim the positive, life affirming, humorous side of Jesus' nature and include this element in worship and ministry. When humor is easily present in a worship setting we will discover . . .

- *A fuller understanding of Christ's nature.*
- *A greater participation of our own range of emotions in worship.*
- *The uniting and binding effect resulting in a deeper sense of fellowship and belonging.*
- *A release from an over-emphasis on solemnity.*
- *A new dimension to prayer.*
- *A richer understanding of the Trinity.*
- *An opportunity to be forgiven for our misuse of this gift and resolve to be more gracious in our application of humor.*

It serves well to recall that the harshest words spoken by Jesus were directed towards those who took themselves so seriously they could not perceive that it was their very attitude to righteousness that became their greatest sin. They became so serious they could no longer laugh at themselves, at their world, or with God. They robbed life and worship of all joy, delight, comic spirit, and humor making religion into a joyless burden often policed by each other.

Humor is a fragile, spiritual and divine gift and in the spirit of worship often refreshes us with the ability to laugh at our foibles, join in a greater sense of connection, and be touched by some gentle healing forces of positive good.

The following worship materials include litanies, a prayer, passages of scripture, hymn, choral and music suggestions, sermon outlines. These are meant as springboards for your own creative ideas.

Litany Of Thanks For All Good Humor And Abiding Joy

Pastor: For all pure comedy and laughter, and for the gift of humor and the comic spirit;
Glory be to thee, O Lord.

People: **For all that which makes us laugh at ourselves, and brings life into perspective;**
Glory be to thee, O Lord.

Pastor: For the spirit of humor which binds us to our neighbor in the joy of laughing together;
Glory be to thee, O Lord.

People: **For the truth that humor brings to our lives, gently reminding us of our frailty and foibles;**
Glory be to thee, O Lord.

Pastor: For all redeeming humor that saves us from taking ourselves and our projects too seriously;
Glory be to thee, O Lord.

People: **For all singers and musicians, for all who work in form and color to increase the joy of life;**
Glory be to thee, O Lord.

Pastor: For all who serve thee with mirth, and cheer, and gladness, and joyfulness;
Glory be to thee, O Lord.

People: **For all who serve men and women by joining mirth with charity, humor with healing, and comedy with truth;**
Glory be to thee, O Lord.

Pastor: For all joy that heightens our lives, kindles our hearts, and enhances our faces with a smile;
Glory be to thee, O Lord.

**People: For the good news of the Gospel that lifts the burden of the heart and brings the merriment of reconciliation;
Glory be to thee, O Lord.**

Rev. Lee van Rensburg
October 1987

The Misuse Of Humor — A Litany Of Confession

Pastor: We confess before God, and before each other that on occasion we have misused the good gift of humor and have caused hurt and humiliation in others.

People: Forgive us for all laughter that has been corrupt, for ridicule and scorn, for mockery and sarcasm, for jibes and derision.

O God, giver of every good gift, forgive our sin.

Pastor: Forgive us for all jokes that have demeaned another race, belittled the opposite sex, or have taken unfair advantage of others.

O God, giver of every good gift, forgive our sin.

People: Forgive us for all humor that has been uncouth, that has traded integrity for a moment of applause, that has made the honorable to be trivial.

O God, giver of every good gift, forgive our sin.

Pastor: May those whom we have laughed at, embarrassed, and hurt with insensitive and aggressive humor be able to forgive us.

We pray for their healing, O God, giver of every good gift.

People: When we have been unwilling to laugh at ourselves, when we have taken ourselves far too seriously, and when we have suppressed the comic spirit in others by our poor attitudes and intimidating moods —

O God, giver of every good gift,
forgive our sin.

Pastor: O God, who in Jesus Christ not only forgives our sin, but provides the way to healing, health and wholesomeness, grant that the good gift of humor may be renewed within us, bringing joy and delight to ourselves and others.

People: O God, who has given us every good gift, grant us charity with our mirth, love with our laughter, and cheerfulness in our work, that we may serve thee with glad mirth all the days of our life, through Christ our Lord.

Amen.

Rev. Lee van Rensburg
November 1987

A Litany Of Thanks
Celebrating The Joy, Mirth, And Gladness
In Holy Scripture

Pastor: For the God who caused Sarah to laugh, for those who heard and laughed with her, and for the child named Isaac — the son of laughter. (Genesis 21:6)

We give you thanks, O Lord.

People: **For the psalmist who wrote of God laughing in the heavens and sporting with Leviathan upon the seas. (Psalm 2:4)**

We give you thanks, O Lord.

Pastor: For the joy of the prophet Isaiah, who wrote, "How beautiful upon the mountains are the feet of Him that bringeth good tidings and publishes peace" (Isaiah 52:7).

We give you thanks, O Lord.

People: **For the angelic host that brough glad tidings of great joy for all mankind (Luke 2:14).**

We give you thanks, O Lord.

Pastor: For the first miracle of our Lord at Cana of Galilee changing water into wine, promising to make the flow of life sparkle (John 2).

We give you thanks, O Lord.

People: **For the good news of the gospel that lifts the burden from the heart and causes the soul to rejoice and sing.**

We give you thanks, O Lord.

Pastor: For the comic spirit in the teachings of Jesus, seeing figs on thistle plants and camels in cups (Matthew 23:24).

We give you thanks, O Lord.

People: **For the father of the returning son who killed the fatted calf and made music and dancing upon his son's safe return (Luke 15).**

We give you thanks, O Lord.

Pastor: For the joy of resurrection that conquers without meeting evil with evil, but overcomes evil with good (Romans 12).

We give you thanks, O Lord.

People: **For the apostle Paul who could find love, joy and peace in being a fool for Christ's sake (1 Corinthians 4:10).**

We give you thanks, O Lord.

Pastor: For the promise of the return of Christ and the great feast and festival at the end of the age.

We give you thanks, O Lord, creator, redeemer and spirit of all joy.

All: **Gloria Patri.**

Rev. Lee van Rensburg
November 1987

The Daughters Of Joy
A Litany Of Thanks For A Gift Of The Spirit

Pastor: We give thanks for the gifts of the Spirit, especially for the gift of inner joy and for all the daughters of joy.

People: **For the daughter called gladness which delights in the good news of other people, and events that bless them.**
We give you thanks, O God.

Pastor: For the daughter called **song** which comes from the heart's overflowing and desire to sing with gusto.
We give you thanks, O God.

People: **For the daughter called cheer which seeks the downcast and helps to raise the sad spirit to liveliness.**
We give you thanks, O God.

Pastor: For the daughter called **rejoicing** that is able to keep a noble spirit in moments of persecution or suffering.
We give you thanks, O God.

People: **For the daughter called merriment that is able to receive the goodness of life, its festivities, celebrations, and anniversaries with music and dancing.**
We give you thanks, O God.

Pastor: For the daughter called **mirth** that is able to see the funny side of life and to laugh at oneself.
We give you thanks, O God.

People: **For the daughter called happiness that finds contentment of spirit in peace with thee, with all the saints and deep within.**
We give you thanks, O God.

Pastor: For the gift of **joy** and all her daughters for gladness and song, cheer and rejoicing, merriment and mirth and happines within, we give you thanks, O God, giver of every good and perfect gift.

Amen.

Rev. Lee van Rensburg
January 1988

A Prayer
For All Gracious Laughter

We give thanks,
for all laughter that fills body and soul
with a sense of well being
making us glad to be part of this good world you have made.

We give thanks,
for all laughter that draws us out of isolation
and merges our soul with those who laugh with us
making us in that moment truly one.

We give thanks
for all laughter that drives out fear
especially for the laughter
of the great cloud of witnesses
who laugh now
over their once so serious fears of death.

We give thanks,
for all laughter that gently reveals
our foibles and falling short
and in that moment kindly beckons us
to character growth and change for the better.

Especially do we give thanks
for all laughter we learn from the Lord
Who brings salvific truth to us through
comic exaggeration, contradictions,
and the colorful characters of the parables.

O Lord,
for all that laughter accomplishes within us
by the Spirit of holiness,
We offer our thanks to thee

from whom comes every good
and perfect gift.

Amen.

> Rev. Lee van Rensburg
> Summer, 1990

A Fool's Prayer

Father and God of Fools, Lord of Clowns and Smiling Saints, I rejoice in this playful prayer, that You are a God of laughter and of tears.

Blessed are You, for You have rooted within me, the gifts of humor, lightheartedness and mirth.
With jokes and comedy; You cause my heart to sing as laughter is made to flow out of me.

I am grateful that your Son, Jesus, who was this world's master of wit, daily invites me to be a fool for Your sake, to embrace the madness of Your prophets, holy people and saints.

I delight in that holy madness which becomes the very medicine to heal the chaos of the cosmos since it calls each of us out of the hum-drumness of daily life into joy, adventure, and most of all, into freedom.

I, who am so easily tempted to barter my freedom for tiny speckles of honor and power, am filled with gratitude that Your Son's very life has reminded me to value only love, the communion with other persons and with you, and to balance honor with humor.

With circus bands and organ grinders, with fools, clowns, court-jesters and comics, with high-spirited angels and saints, I too join the fun and foolishness of life, so that Your holy laughter may ring out to the edges of the universe.

by Rev. Edward M. Hays[1]

---

[1] Used by permission from Forest of Peace Books, Inc., Easton, KS.

Hymns, Anthems, And Music Appropriate For Use In Services With A Humor Theme

Hymns

Hymn No. 57 — O For a Thousand Tongues to Sing
             Tune — Azmon

Hymn No. 75 — All People That On Earth Do Dwell
             Tune — Old Hundredth
             ("Serve Him with **mirth**")

Hymn No. 89 — Joyful, Joyful, We Adore Thee
             Tune — Hymn to Joy

Hymn No. 144 — This Is My Father's World
              Tune — Terra Beta

Hymn No. 224 — Good Christian Friends, Rejoice
              Tune — In Dulci Jublio

Hymn No. 261 — Lord of the Dance
              Tune — Lord of the Dance

Hymn No. 421 — Make Me a Captive, Lord
              Tune — Diademata
              (Paradoxes)

Hymn No. 611 — Child of Blessing, Child of Promise
              Tune — Stuttgart
              ("Grow to **laugh**, and sing, and worship")

Hymn No. 715 — Rejoice, the Lord Is King
              Tune — Darwall's 148th

All the above references are from the *The United Methodist Hymnal* (Nashville: The Methodist Publshing House, 1989.)

Also:

Hymn No. 132 — Holy Ghost, Dispel Our Sadness
            Tune — Hyfrydol

Hymn No. 231 — Sometimes A Light Surprises
            Tune — Llanfyllin

Hymn No. 378 — God Rest You Merry, Gentlemen
            Tune — God Rest You

These hymns are from *The Methodist Hymnal* (Nashville: The Methodist Publishing House, 1966.)

Organ Preludes

Musette — Gounod
Siciliano — Scarlatti
Gig — Ziropoli
Sonata No. 3 for Violin & Organ — G. F. Handel

Choir Introits

For the Beauty of the Earth — Dix
Awake My Soul and with the Sun — Tallis

Interludes

Cantabile — Paldini

Anthems

My Dancing Day — arr. Robert Shaw
All Poor Men and Humble — English Traditional
Immortal Love, Forever Full — Eugene Butler
Old Hundredth Psalm Tune — by R. Vaughan Williams
Praise the Lord, His Glories Show — G. F. Handel

Organ Postludes

Beethoven's Fifth, theme, the 1st movement
                                        — L. von Beethoven
Beethoven's Ninth, theme, 4th movement
                                        — L. von Beethoven
Grand March — Stickles
Allegro Grandisoso — Stickles
Caprice — Wely

Some Forms Of Humor With Scriptural Reference

LAUGHTER
"And Sarah said, God hath made me to laugh; every one that heareth will laugh with me" (Genesis 21:6).

DIVINE LAUGHTER
"He that sitteth in the heavens shall laugh: The Lord shall have them in derision" (Psalm 2:4).

CHRIST AND LAUGHTER
"Blessed are ye that hunger now: for ye shall be filled. Blessed are ye that weep now: for ye shall laugh" (Luke 6:21).

FOOLS FOR CHRIST'S SAKE
"We are fools for Christ's sake, but ye are wise in Christ; we are weak, but ye are strong; ye have glory, but we have dishonor" (1 Corinthians 4:10).

COMIC REVERSAL
"I say unto you, This man went down to his house justified rather than the other: for every one that exalteth himself shall be humbled; but he that humbleth himself shall be exalted" (Luke 18:14).

HYPERBOLE
"Or how wilt thou say to thy brother, Let me cast out the mote out of thine eye; and lo, the beam is in thine own eye" (Matthew 7:4)?

"And again I say unto you, It is easier for a camel to go through a needle's eye, than for a rich man to enter into the kingdom of God" (Matthew 19:24).

IRONY
"And Nathanael said unto him, Can any good thing come out of Nazareth? Philip saith unto him, Come and see" (John 1:45).

"Woe unto you, scribes and Pharisees, hyprocrites! for ye build the sepulchers of the prophets, and garnish the tombs of the righteous" (Matthew 23:29).

PARADOXES
"But many shall be last that are first; and first that are last" (Matthew 19:30).
"He that findeth his life shall lose it; and he that loseth his life for my sake shall find it" (Matthew 10:39).

PUN
"And Samson said, with the jaw-bone of an **ass**,
I have plied them in a **mass**.
With the jaw-bone of an **ass**
I have **ass**ailed **ass**ailants" (Judges 15:16 Moffat).

RIDICULE
(One part of a hewn tree used for household needs and the other part used to carve a god!)
"Then shall it be for a man to burn; and he taketh thereof, and warmeth himself; yea he kindleth it, and baketh bread; yea, he maketh a god, and worshippeth it; he maketh it a graven image, and falleth down thereto" (Isaiah 44:15).

RIDDLE
"And Samson said unto them, Let me now put forth a riddle unto you . . . Out of the eater came forth meat, And out of the strong came forth sweetness" (Judges 14:12, 14).

SATIRE
(The Book of Jonah)

All references from Revised Standard Version except Judges 15:16 which is from the James Moffat translation.

Sermon Suggestions

As an introduction, draw attention to the fact that laughter is not only good for the soul, it is also good for the body. A good laugh is tantamount to a veritable physical workout. It exercises **muscles** (at least 15 different muscles are required to crack a smile); the **lungs** rapidly inhale and exhale during a hearty laugh; the **larynx and voice box** exert themselves in a wide range of sounds; the **heart** receives an aerobic workout as it is called upon to beat more rapidly and provide blood and oxygen for the physical parts already involved; the **thorax and diaphragm** expand and retract; and besides all this some go so far as to "roll in the aisles," and "double up" among other contortions introduced by laughter. If you can't jog or play tennis, a good comedy once a week should do the trick!

The comic spirit given to us is first present in the Creator, the Christ, and the Spirit. Each aspect of the divine nature reveals something of this quality and in the creation the gift flows from heaven to earth, from the divine nature to mother nature reaching its highest reflection in human nature. "God has made me to laugh" (Genesis 21:6)

Humor And The Creator

"The Lord created Leviathen to play in the seas"
(Psalm 104:26)

The comic spirit is everywhere evident in the created order. A popular song draws attention to, "green alligators and long necked geese, humpty back camels and chimpanzees." The animal world in its natural state as well as in captivity (zoo, circus) is filled with natural comedy . . . bouncing kangaroos, wobbling penguins, ribbet frogs, spouting whales, and the ever amusing antics of orangutans and the monkey family.

The cartoon world unashamedly draws from this natural comedy allowing us to laugh at our foibles in animal characters.

Daffy Duck, Mickey Mouse, Yogi Bear, Road Runner and Coyote, Tweety and Sylvester, Woody Woodpecker, Donald Duck, Goofy . . . the list is seemingly endless. This inherent comedy in creation is recognized by us because God has placed within us the gift of humor which comes from his own image and likeness. It is indeed true that, "God has made me to laugh so that all who hear shall laugh with me" (Genesis 21:6).

Humor And The Christ

"It is meet that we should be merry" (Luke 15:32)

Christians have always affirmed that Jesus shares a full human nature with us in his incarnation. A Jesus without a sense of humor would be a strange example of human nature! It is this very sense of humor that is one of the differentiating features between ourselves and the animals and draws attention to "the image and likeness of God" given to the human spirit. Jesus surely expressed mirth and humor as he joined in the camaraderie of the disciples that traveled with him up and down the length and breadth of Galilee.

His teaching evidences a humorous element, comic exaggeration, comic reversal, irony, paradoxes and much more (see pages 24-27) as he dealt with the ambiguities, incongruities and contradictions of life that cropped up from day to day.

His promise was to bring laughter to those who were poor, downtrodden, sick, prisoners and oppressed, "and those who weep now shall know laughter in the kingdom of God" (Luke 6:21).

Humor And The Spirit

"He will guide you in truth" (John 16:13)

One work of the Spirit is to convince us of God's gift of humor within and guide us to a responsible and mature appreciation and use of this gift. Humor being a gift of spirit is susceptible to corruption in the form of derision, scoffing, scorn, sarcasm, jibing, mockery, ridicule and all forms that seek to embarrass, hurt, wound, take advantage, or put down another. Misused (sinful) humor can be derogatory, abusive, aggressive, poke fun of, and hurt others. Certain Ethnic and "dirty jokes" may come into the same misuse of this God-given gift.

The spirit leads us to confess our sin in this area, to use our gift in responsible ways. The spirit uses humor to gently lead us to truth concerning ourselves and in the ability to laugh at our own foibles, salvation and redemption of a form are introduced to us. We may also see truth in a new way for all humor is based on truth. It may well increase our compassion and keep us in better health.

Humor In Heaven

"You shall know laughter in the Kingdom of God" (Luke 6:21)

It seems that humor is meant for God and man, for heaven and earth and that the place where humor is found missing is none other than hell itself. Dante in his work, *The Divine Comedy*, after leading us through the lower regions of hell, leading us up the torturous path through purgatory brings us to the gates of the celestial palaces with these words, "It was a sound I had not heard before. I stopped and listened. It sounded like the laughter of the universe."

Hell is boring. No laughter, joy, merriment, stifling life itself. Merriment and laughter are to be found in people God has touched, in the followers of Christ, in the midst of their fellowship and worship. The rightful place for mirth is in the kingdom of God in the hearts of men and women who have responded to his light, life and love and confess that it is indeed, "God who has made me to laugh so that all who hear shall laugh with me."

Church Programs And Adult Forums That Use Humor

I have selected the following three programs from several that were used in our church at Whitehouse, New Jersey. These programs were well received and are easily adaptable.

A: TRUTH IN CARTOONS

Cartoons are one of the most vivid expressions of truth. Cartoonists are shrewd observers of our society and culture, our religious lives, our politicians and leaders and the many incongruities of our lives. This is presented in a palatable form helping us laugh at ourselves, and change. Many cartoons have an undeniably theological presupposition and reflect our understanding and perception of God. This program is designed to look particularly at the scripture, theology and church life and an abundance of cartoons are available for such use.

Cartoons that are selected are easily transferred onto transparencies and with the use of an overhead projector that is about all one needs. Cartoons that are most useful for this kind of presentation are those of Charles Schulz (Peanuts), Doug Marlette (Rev. Will. B. Dunn), Doonesbury, Bringing up Father to mention a few. Those present for the presentation enjoy the cartoons and are able to contribute their understanding of the truth and presuppositions behind the cartoons. Normally only 10 to 15 cartoons are necessary to fill up an hour.

Two cartoon examples follow . . .

The first cartoon by Kavanagh and Johnson (Reprinted with special permission of King Features Syndicate.) opens a discussion on, Does one have to be caught to be punished? What constitutes punishment? Do we punish ourselves? Are we more severe in judging ourselves than God? Is it easier to forgive ourselves or others?

Cartoon two, by Doug Marlette, (Reprinted with permission of Peachtree Publishers.) leads into a discusion on popular preaching. Was Jesus a popular preacher? Do we have to accommodate our proclamation in order to secure a hearing?

An excellent source for cartoons which easily lead into theological discussion and open issues on morality, ethics and Christian living can be located in Robert Short's two books, *The Gospel According to Peanuts* (John Knox Press) and *The Parables of Peanuts* (Harper & Row). Charles Schulz provides the cartoons and Robert Short the comment.

For instance, in one cartoon Lucy tells Linus that she and Patty are planning a picnic for the next day and that she "hopes to goodness" that it doesn't rain. Linus wonders whether hoping to goodness is theologically sound. Is it? Are we all theologians at one level or another?

In yet another cartoon by Schulz Lucy says to Charlie Brown, "You reap what you sow! You get out of life exactly what you put into it. No more and no less!!" Snoopy overhearing this statement reflects, "I'd like to see a little more margin for error!" This cartoon lets us talk about the apparent contradiction between this scriptural statement and forgiveness and mercy. How do we resolve the issue of sowing and reaping (karma) and our debts being forgiven?

This kind of program helps to recognize the underlying issues of morality, scripture, theology, ethics and life's incongruities that often are the basis of the cartoon.

B: HEALING AND HUMOR

A video tape presentation by Norman Cousins (author of An Anatomy of an Illness) is available called, Anatomy of an Illness: The Healing Power of Humor. This may be obtained from Penrose Productions, 1042 Hamilton Court, Menlo Park, CA 94025, Phone (415) 323-TAPE.

The 43 minute tape is an excellent introduction to the relation between laughter and healing. People suffering from different ailments affirm the positive effect laughter has had on their lives. Norman Cousins tells his own story and guides the discussions. The presentation is witty, thought provoking and points us in the direction of utilizing humor and laughter in our own healing ministries within the local church.

C: HUMOR IN RELATIONSHIP BUILDING

A Serendipity hour may be arranged for developing relationships within existing church groups and committees, to help assimilate new members into the church, and to build greater levels of trust and facilitate better understanding and communication.

Responding to situations like, "Who among those present this morning would you like to be trapped in an elevator with and why?" provide lighthearted and humorous responses that offer personal information about those present in playful and delightful ways that are uplifting. Many relationships are initiated, cemented or enhanced by this opportunity under the umbrella of serendipidic mirth.

Serendipity material is available from: Serendipity House, Box 1012, Littleton, Colorado 80160. Phone: 1-800-525-9563.

A fourth program has been designed, though not yet executed in our local church. It is called *Humor and History* and plans to invite senior members of the church to share humorous anecdotes from past years and former pastors with the rest of the congregation. This could take place at a covered dish supper or some other appropriate gathering. The relating of their humorous accounts of past events is designed to facilitate relations between long time and new members and to increase a sense of "shared history."

A series of programs on humor can be productive in the life of the church raising levels of consciousness, appreciation, and understanding of the wide range and use of humor in service of the church and as spiritual strength to Christian living and ministry.

Chapter 5

A HUMOR PROFILE FOR YOUR CHURCH

The average church keeps reference files on membership, finances, annual reports and the like. However, more and more churches are expanding their reference material to include local demographics, population shifts, cultural trends and projected needs of the community (e.g. day care, baby boomers.) A useful profile to have on hand is that of a church humor profile. This profile would reveal the nature, source, level, use and effect of humor in church life, worship and organization structure. Laughter is generally present where people gather. It can tell us a great deal more than whether people are simply having a good time. For instance, it is an indicator of the level of mutual trust and facilitating presence of good leadership. The lack of, or low level of humor can warn of possible problems. A humor profile is designed to reveal:
1. The amount of humor present (minimal, frequent, abundant) and can be correlated with the willingness to be present and the likely level of productivity.
2. The source of the humor (pastor, chairperson, single or multiple sources).
3. The nature of the humor (positive, negative, aggressive, inclusive, exclusive). The hidden agenda is as significant as the printed one.
4. The kinds of humor (wit, pun, mimic).
5. The effects of humor (distracting, facilitating, accommodating, providing a sense of well being.)

From data collected on the following evaluation sheets an interesting profile begins to emerge revealing insights, patterns, levels, tendencies, needs, and benefits. For instance, a profile revealing that humor is minimally present, exclusive and tending to come only from one source may be correlated with a committee that is difficult to find people to sit on and is generally unproductive. Maybe the organizational structure is too formal, too serious, and the wrong person in the leadership position. It needs to lighten up to become attractive and effective. People avoid this group because their level of comfort is intimidated. A moderate to high level of humor suggests a comfortable social environment, good spirit, friendliness, a sense of well being and acceptance and naturally leads to a more creative and productive meeting. Knowing, rather than guessing or presuming where the levels are, can be a useful tool at the time nominations come around.

Using the data sheets provided and designed for gathering a humor profile the following factors should be taken into account.

1. Do not let the size of the gathering be of consequence. If the gathering is small that's okay. It may in fact be used to indicate whether humor tends to be correlated with numbers in your church or not. (Is humor contingent on more or less people present?)

2. Use the data sheet for several of the same meetings. A one-time data gathering is inadvisable. The more numerous the occasions the more accurate the profile for that group.

3. Ask at least two people (preferably different in gender, age, outlook) to complete the data sheet after the meeting. This helps provide objectivity.

4. Data gathering should be discreet. If everyone knows what is happening then the humor may well be contrived. A subtle, low profile approach to monitoring the level of humor present will provide a better index.

5. It is preferable to undertake this kind of project at a high activity time of the year rather than, say, the summer time. The temptation is to execute this kind of project at a convenient time rather than a busy time but it is just the very nature of the busy time that will give us the profile that is most useful to us.

The profile may be composed of individual meetings (boards, councils, trusts, evangelism, finance, education, and especially the worship service) and then compiled into a general church profile.

The project may be easily managed. Appoint a person to chair the project; copy the forms included in this book; give them to those elected to collect the data; afterwards collate and analyze the data; make an overall profile; share profile with groups and church via newsletter etc.; keep on file for reference. This should greatly contribute to the appreciation and understanding of the presence and function of humor in your church life.

After running a humor profile at WUMC we discovered that humor was a greater part of our being together than we first believed. We became more alert to its presence and contribution in worship (via music, hymn, scripture), we moved toward a more responsible use of personal humor with greater understanding of its affect on others, and we are learning to utilize it positively within the other ministries of our church.

Humor In Church Gatherings

NAME OF FUNCTION/MEETING/EVENT

DATE: _____

TIME: MORNING/AFTERNOON/EVENING _____

NUMBER PRESENT: _____

Note: Check (x) all boxes that apply.

PRESENCE

1. Was humor present at function/meeting/event?
   Yes ☐ No ☐

2. If yes, was it — minimal ☐ frequent ☐ or abundant? ☐

3. Was humor predominantly before ☐ during ☐ or after ☐ the function? Or was it more or less evenly interspersed? ☐

SOURCE

4. Was humor contributed by same person ☐ or different persons? ☐

5. Was humor contributed by male ☐ female ☐, senior ☐, youth ☐, chairperson ☐, pastor? ☐

6. How many occasions can you recall? _____
   Approximate? _____

NATURE

7. Was humor generally inclusive? ☐

8. Was it ever exclusive? ☐

9. Was it spontaneous? ☐

10. Was any humor in your opinion contrived/forced? ☐

11. Was it manipulative? ☐

12. Was it generally good-natured/kind? ☐

13. Was anyone ever embarrassed? ☐ Was any humor in poor taste? ☐

14. Was it isolated? ☐ Or did it tend to generate 3 or 4 responses? ☐

FORM

Were you able to recognize any of these forms of humor?

Positive		Negative
Joke ☐	Exaggeration ☐	Ridicule ☐
Jest ☐	Reversal ☐	Scorn ☐
Wit ☐	Quip ☐	Sarcasm ☐
Pun ☐	Irony ☐	Contempt ☐
Clowning ☐	Ridiculous ☐	Mocking ☐

Other _____

EFFECT

15. Was the effect generally positive? ☐

16. Was any of the humor negative? ☐

17. Was any of the humor helpful ☐, distracting ☐, disruptive ☐, facilitating ☐, intimidating ☐, helpful in releasing tension ☐, amusing ☐?

HUMOR AS MINISTRY

18. Did humor contribute to any of these areas?

    Group esprit d' corps ☐

    Healing/therapeutic ☐

    Spiritual insight ☐

    Cause self-reflection ☐

    Learning ☐

    Relationships ☐

    Sense of well being ☐

COMMENTS
Form completed by:

_____

_____

Humor Sunday
Evaluation Sheet

1. On a scale of 1 (low) to 10 (high), how meaningful was the service to you this morning? _____

2. Did you learn anything new about humor? Yes ☐ No ☐

3. In which parts of the service were you conscious of humor/cheer/joy/mirth?
   Hymns ☐   Prayers ☐
   Sermon ☐   Children's Time ☐
   Litany ☐   Affirmation ☐
   Scripture ☐   Announcements ☐
   Anthem/Choir ☐   Music ☐

4. Was there a message for you concerning your own use of humor? Yes ☐ No ☐

5. Do you feel comfortable with laughter in the sanctuary? Yes ☐ No ☐

6. Were you offended at all at any point? Yes ☐ No ☐

7. Do you think that Jesus has a sense of humor and laughed on occasion? Yes ☐ No ☐

8. Do you perceive humor as a spiritual gift? Yes ☐ No ☐

9. Where was humor most helpful? Fellowship ☐ Learning ☐ Spiritual Insight ☐

10. In your opinion, is humor an effective vehicle for truth about ourselves? Yes ☐ No ☐

11. What was most meaningful for you today?

Please use the rest of this sheet for any additional comments, insights, observations or remarks you may wish to make.

Thank you for the time you took to complete this evaluation sheet. I appreciate it.

EPILOGUE

Humor and the comic spirit offers a refreshing and sustaining ministry to us on our Christian pilgrimage. It is not only a gift we receive from God, but a gift we have to give each other, and like most spiritual gifts it may be kept while given away. Like trying to catch a butterfly, humor is elusive and this may be its strength. When we intentionally grasp it seeking to analyze, manipulate or contrive, it flees from us. While we look elsewhere it settles on us and gently refreshes us with its charm. Let us seek not to understand humor too deeply, too often, or for too long. It is most refreshing when it steals on us with surprise, like the journey on the Emmaus road, calls us to reflect afterwards, "Did not our hearts burn within us as we journeyed on the way" (Luke 24:32)?

Appendix A

Bimonthly Publication On Humor

The Fellowship of Merry Christians
P.O. Box 668
Kalamazoo, MI 49005-0668

This organization offers a bi-monthly newsletter called "The Joyful Noiseletter," posters of the smiling/laughing Christ, and available resources on humor research. Membership is open to both clergy and lay persons. The definitive statement at the head of the Newsletter offers, "Our modest aim is to recapture the spirit of joy, humor, unity and healing power of the early Christians. We try to be merry more than twice a year. The opinions expressed in this newsletter are not always those of God."

Appendix B

At the fifth annual conference of the Institute of Advancement of Human Behavior, held in Boston, Massachusetts in September, 1987, the theme for the three-day conference was *The Power of Laughter and Play*, linking humor directly with health, creativity, the reduction of stress, and better living patterns. Title of the lectures and workshops included, "Laugh Your Way to Health," "The Power of Humor in the Work Environment," "Humor and Health," and "Stress Management and Humor."

Lecturers and workshop leaders included: Annette Goodheart, Ph.D., a psychotherapist in private practice in Santa Barbara, California; Joel Goodman, Ed.D., Director of The Humor Project at Saratoga Institute in Saratoga Springs, New York; Allison B. Crane, B.S.N., R.N., President of Crane Consultants, a firm which helps health care agencies improve the patient's environment through compassion and humor; and Steve Allen Jr., M.D., a practicing family physician. He is Clinical Instructor at the Upstate Medical Center School of Medicine in Syracuse, New York.

Appendix C

FORMS OF HUMOR AND THE COMIC SPIRIT

Buffoonery	Paradox
Cartoons	Parody
Caricature	Pun
Derision	Quip
Farce	Repartee
Hyperbole	Riddle
Impersonation	Ridicule
Irony	Sarcasm
Jesting	Satire
Joke	Scoffing
Lampoon	Spoonerism
Ludicrous	Travesty
Malapropism	Wit
Mockery	

BIBLIOGRAPHY

Adams, Douglas G. "Humor in the American Pulpit from George Whitfield Through Henry Ward Beecher." Th.D. Dissertation, Theological Union.

———. "The Place of Humor in Preaching and Worship." *Preaching and Worship* (1980):142-146.

Aichele, George. *Theology as Comedy: Critical and Theoretical Implications.* Washington D.C.: University Press of America, 1980.

Alexander, John. "Christopher Fry and Religious Comedy." *Meanjion* XV (Autumn 1956):77-81.

Berger, Peter L. *A Rumor of Angels: Modern Society and the Rediscovery of the Supernatural.* Garden City, New York: Doubleday-Anchor, 1970.

Bergson, Henri. "Laughter." *Comedy* --- New York: Doubleday Anchor Books, 1956:61-90.

Bessiere, Gerard. "Humor — A Theological Attitude." *Theology of Joy* (1974):81-95.

Bishop, John. "Let Your Humor Shine." *Circuit Rider* (June 1986):3.

Bohren, Rudolf. "Kleiner Exkurs uber Predigt und Humor." *Der Glaube Der* (1969):60-67.

Boonstra, Harry. "Satire in Matthew." *Christianity and Literature* 29 (Summer 1980):32-45.

Branson, R. "And Now . . . The Theology of Joy." *Encounter* 34 (Summer 1973):233-245.

Brown, Robert McAfee. "The Spirit's Eighth Gift." *Christianity and Crisis* 40 (February 4, 1980):8-10.

Brill, A. A., ed. *The Basic Writings of Sigmund Freud.* New York: Modern Library, 1938.

Buechner, Frederick. *Telling the Truth: The Gospel as Tragedy, Comedy & Fairy Tale.* San Francisco: Harper & Row, 1975.

Bullard, John Moore. "Biblical Humor — Its Nature and Function." Ph.D. Dissertation, Yale University, 1962.

Cox, Harvey. *The Feast of Fools.* Massachusetts: Harvard University Press, 1969.

Craddock, Fred. *As One Without Authority.* Nashville: Abingdon Press, 1986.

Crossan, John. *Raid on the Articulate: Comic Eschatology in Jesus and Borges.* New York: Harper & Row, 1976.

Danker, F. W. "Laughing with God." *Christianity Today* 11 (January 6, 1967):16-18.

Davenport, Gary T. "Elliot's The Cocktail Party: Comic Persepctive as Salvation." *Modern Drama* 17, No. 3 (Summer 1974):301-306.

Davies, J. G. "Worship and Humor." *Research Bulletin* 1975:3-9.

Deuser, Hermann. "Humor and Christentum." *Evangelische Theologie* 37 (November-December, 1977):588-590.

Duke, Paul D. *Irony in the Fourth Gospel*. Atlanta: John Knox, 1985.

Eastman, Max. *The Sense of Humor*. New York: Max Scribner & Sons, 1921.

Feibleman, James. *In Praise of Comedy*. New York, 1939.

Fisher, Eugene J. "Divine Comedy — Humor in the Bible." *Religious Education* 72 (November-December 1977):571-579.

Freud, Sigmund. *Jokes and their Relation to the Unconscious*. New York: W. W. Norton, 1963.

Garrett, Graeme. "My Brother Essau Is An Hairy Man: An Encounter between the Comedian and the Preacher." *Scottish Journal of Theology* 33 (1980):239-256.

Gevirtz, Stanley. "Of Patriarchs and Puns." *Hebrew Union College Annual* 46 (1975):33-54.

Gill, Jerry. "Jesus, Irony and the New Quest." Encounter 41 (1980):139-151.

Gluck, J. J. "Paronomasia in Biblical Literature." *Semitics* 1 (1978):50-78.

Good, Edwin M. *Irony in the Old Testament*. Philadelphia: Westminster, 1965.

Greeley, Andrew M. "Humor and Ecclesiastical Ministry." *Theology of Joy* (1974):134-140.

Hamilton, K. and Haverluck, R. T. "Laughter and Vision." *Soundings* 55 (Summer 1972):163-177.

Harris, Marie. "Religious Educators and the Comic Vision." *Religious Education* 75 (July-August 1980):422-432.

Hayes, Bert. "A Study of Humor in the Old Testament." Ph.D. Dissertation, Hebrew Union College, 1964.

Heflin, James Larohn. "An Evaluation of the Use of Humor in the Sermon." Th.D. Dissertation, South Western Baptist Theological Seminary, 1974.

Holmer, P. L. "Something About What Makes It Funny." *Soundings* 57 (Summer 1974):157-174.

Hunter, Edward Gordon. "Humor in the Pulpit." D.Min. Dissertation, School of Theology at Claremont, 1978.

Hussey, L. M. "The Wit of the Carpenter." *The American Mercury* V (July 1925):329-336.

Hyers, Conrad. "Comedy and Creation." *Theology Today* 39 (April 1982):17-26.

———— "The Dialect of the Sacred and the Comic." *Cross Currents* 19, 1969.

———— *And God Created Laughter*. Atlanta: John Knox, 1987.

———— *Zen and the Comic Spirit*. Philadelphia: Westminster, 1973.

———— *The Comic Vision and the Christian Faith*. New York: Pilgrim Press, 1981.

———— *Holy Laughter: Essays on Religion in the Comic Perspective*. New York: Seabury, 1969.

Ice, J. L. "Notes Toward a Theology of Humor." *Religion in Life* 42 (Autumn 1973):388-400.

Koestler, Arthur. *The Act of Creation*. New York: The MacMillan Company, 1964.

Krause, George E. "The Humor of the Heilgeschichte." *Concordia Journal* 7, No. 1 (January 1981):21-23.

Lang, D. B. "On the Biblical Comic." *Judaism* 11, (Summer 1962):249-254.

Levine, Jacob. "Response to Humor." *Scientific American* 194, 1956.

Lohfink, Gerhard. *The Bible Now I Get It*. New York: Doubleday & Company, 1979.

Lys, Daniel. "Alchimie du Verbe et Demythisation. (note sur l'humour Biblique)" *Maggel Shagedh: La Branche D'Amandier* (1960):114-126.

McGhee, Paul and Goldstein, Jeffery. *Handbook on Humor Research*. New York: Springer Verlag, 1983.

McLelland, Joseph C. *The Clown and the Crocodile*. Atlanta: John Knox Press, 1970.

———— "Comedy — Human and Divine." *The Church in the Modern World* (1967):273:287.

———— "The Doxology as Suspension of the Tragic." *Theology Today* 32 (July 1974):114-120.

Meier, George Friedrich. *Thoughts on Jesting*. Austin, Texas: University of Texas Press, 1947.

Meredith, George. "An Essay on Comedy." *Comedy--* New York: Doubleday Anchor Books, 1956 pp. 3-61.

Miller, David L. "Salvation and the Image of Comedy: Pirandello & Aristophanes." *Religion in Life* (Summer 1964):451-466.

Mindess, Harvey. *Laughter and Liberation*. Los Angeles: Nash, 1971.

Morrison, Dudley. *The Humor of Christ*. London: ---, 1931.

Mueller, W. R. "God's Fools: Biblical and Modern." *Theology Today* 23 (January 1967):538-550.

Mullen, W. H. "Toward a Theology of Humor (with a response by Dr. Anderson)" *Christian Scholass Review* 3, No. 1 (1973):3-14.

Nicholls, S. Thomas. "The Comic Vision and the Stories of David." *Encounter* 42, (1981):277-283.

Niehbur, Reinhold. *Discerning the Signs of the Times*. New York: Charles Scribner & Sons, 1946.

Nielson, C. M. "How to Teach the Doctrine of the Trinity in an Age of Academic and Social Disorder." *Religion in Life* 43, (Autumn 1974):306-311.

Oden, Thomas. *The Living God*. New York: Harper & Row, 1987.

Parrill, Lloyd. "Concept of Humor in the Pseudonymous Works of Soren Kierkegaard." (Dissertation Abstract) *Drew Gateway* 46 (1975/76):116-117.

Parrot, Bob W. "Biblical Preaching and the Use of Humor." D. Min. Dissertation, Southern Methodist University, 1977.

_____. "Evangelism with a Sense of Humor." *Forward* 3, (September 1982):1-4.

_____. "Ontology of Humor: A Basis for Biblical Exegesis." *Perkins Journal* 32 (Fall 1978):14-34.

Potthoff, Harvey. "Humor and Religious Faith." *American Theological Library Association: Proceedings* 34 (1980):74-80.

Ratcliff, John. "Humor as a Religious Experience." Th.D. Dissertation, Southern Baptist Theological Seminary, 1970.

Redding, D. A. "God Made Me to Laugh." *Christianity Today* 6 (July 6, 1982):3-4.

Riegert, E. R. "Parabolic Sermons." *Lutheran Quarterly* 26 (1974).

Rossow, Francis C. "Dramatic Irony in the Bible — with a Difference." *Concordia Journal* 8 (March 1982):48:52.

Saliers, D. E. "Faith and the Comic Eye: Religious Gleanings from Comic Vision in Recent Fiction." *Andover Newton Quarterly* 13 (March 1973):259-276.

Sayward, John. *Perfect Fools: Folly for Christ's Sake in Catholic and Orthodox Spirituality*. New York: Oxford University Press, 1980.

Schiffers, Nobert. "The Humor of John XXIII." *Theology of Joy* (1974):126-133.

Scott, Nathan A., Jr. "The Bias of Comedy and the Narrow Escape into Faith." *The Christian Scholar* XLIV (Spring 1961).

Short, Robert. *The Gospel According to Peanuts*. Great Britain: Collins Fontana Books, 1965.

_____. *The Parables of Peanuts*. Great Britain: Collins Fontana Books, 1969.

Spencer, Ada B. "The Wise Fool (and the Foolish Wise): A Study of Irony in Paul (2 Corinthians 11 vs 16; 12 vs 3.)" *Novum Testamentum* 23 (October 1981):349-360.

Steimle, Edmund; Niedenthal, Morris; and Rice, Charles. *Preaching the Story*. Philadelphia: Fortress Press, 1983.

Stendahl, Krister. *Paul Among Jews and Gentiles*. Philadelphia: Fortress Press, 1986.

Strange, M. "God and Laughter." *Worship* 45 (January 1971):1-12.

Swakey, Marie Collins. *Comic Laughter*. New Haven: Yale University Press, 1961.

Swain, Barbara. *Fools and Folly During the Middle Ages Renaissance*. New York: Columbia University Press, 1932.

Sypher, Wylie. *Comedy*. New York: Doubleday Anchor Books, 1956.

Tanenbaum, Marc H. "Humor in the Talmud." *Theology of Joy* (1974):141-150.

Trueblood, Elton. *The Humor of Christ*. New York: Harper & Row, 1975.

Van der Horst, P. W. "Is Wittiness Unchristian? A Note on Ephesians 5 vs 4." *Miscellanea Neotestamentica* 2 (1978):163-171.

Via, Dan O. *Kerygma and Comedy in the New Testament*. Philadelphia: Fortress Press, 1975.

Von Campenhausen, Hans. "Ein Witz des Apostels Paulus and die Anfange des Christlichen Humors." *Aus der Fruhzeit des Christentums* (1963):102-108.

_____. "Christentum und Humor." *Aus der Fruhzeit des Christentums*. (1963):308-330.

Vos, Nelvin. *For God's Sake Laugh*. Richmond, John Knox Press, 1966.

_____. "Structures of Comedy and the Christian Faith." Ph.D. Dissertation, University of Chicago, 1965.

Vosko, Per. "Kristedom og Humor." *For Herren Vil Vi Bygge* (1962):69-76.

Wardlaw, Don. *Preaching Biblically*. Philadelphia: Westminster Press 1983.

Webster, Gary. *Laughter in the Bible*. St. Louis: Bethany Press, 1960.

Whedbee, William. "The Comedy of Job." *Semeia* 7 (1977):1-39.

Willimon, William. *And the Laugh Shall Be First*. Nashville: Abingdon Press, 1986.

Zuver, Dudley. *Salvation by Laughter*. New York: Harper & Brothers, 1933.